In case of loss, please return to:

_____

_____

_____

_____

As a reward: $_____

AS PART OF OUR COMMITMENT TO BEING RESPONSIBLE STEWARDS, THREADS IS GOING GREEN. *THE TOUGH SAYINGS OF JESUS II* IS THE FIRST THREADS STUDY PRINTED ON 100% RECYCLED PAPER.

THE TOUGH SAYINGS OF JESUS II

MICHAEL KELLEY

Published by LifeWay Press®
© 2008 Michael Kelley

ISBN: 978-1415-8651-94
Item: 005136924

Dewey Decimal Classification Number: 234.2
Subject Heading: JESUS CHRIST—TEACHINGS \ BELIEF AND DOUBT \ FAITH

Printed in the United States of America.

Leadership and Adult Publishing
LifeWay Church Resources
One LifeWay Plaza
Nashville, Tennessee 37234-0175

We believe the Bible has God for its author; salvation for its end; and truth, without
any mixture of error, for its matter and that all Scripture is totally true and trustworthy.
The 2000 statement of The Baptist Faith and Message is our doctrinal guideline.

TABLE OF CONTENTS

MEET THE **AUTHOR**

MY NAME IS MICHAEL KELLEY. I live in Nashville, Tennessee, with my wife, Jana, and our two kids, Joshua and Andi. I grew up in Texas before moving to Birmingham, Alabama, to attend Beeson Divinity School where I earned a Master of Divinity. I work full-time as an editor for *Threads* as well as traveling to teach at events, conferences, and churches across the country.

A little more about me—I love to be entertained and can be found watching way too much television and way too many movies. I'm not cool enough to listen to much music, but I love sports and think that October is the greatest month of the year. I keep meaning to start another degree but I just can't seem to find the right time. I have an unhealthy addiction to fruit-flavored candy.

I learn more and more about the Lord through experiencing how my wife loves me. I also believe that God wants me to communicate stuff I am experiencing with my community, not necessarily stuff that I have a firm grasp on. So thanks for processing the truths in this book alongside of me. I hope these sessions offer you as much anxiety, trouble, fear, apprehension— and hope as they did me. You can come by and visit me online at *michaelkelleyministries.com*.

THE TOUGH SAYINGS OF JESUS II

LIMPING ALONG

"For God so loved the world . . ."

You know the rest. There are some statements that Jesus made that have gotten comfortable for us. They have become like a favorite T-shirt, well-worn and broken in. We put them on because they feel good. They are familiar. We like the way they look—and we should.

"God so loved the world" is no less true today than it was in some back room of a Palestinian house 2,000 years ago when Jesus first said it. God still loves the world. He did give His one and only Son to pave the way for people to come back to Him. That's completely legitimate.

That is, however, not the only thing Jesus said. He said lots of stuff, and much of it isn't quite as easy to wear as that famous verse from John. He called a woman a dog. He told a rich, young ruler that he could work his way to heaven. He said He was glad a good friend of His was dead. It's those words of Jesus that don't fit quite as comfortably as the 3:16 shirt.

But when we neglect the fullness of what Jesus said—when we only think about those things that are comfortable for us to consider—then we are living up to the famous definition

When we only think about those things that are comfortable for us to consider, we are living up to the famous definition that Karl Marx gave to religion in general. In his words, religion is "the opium of the people." We use our religion—in this case, Christianity—to make ourselves feel better.

that Karl Marx gave to religion in general. In his words, religion is "the opium of the people." We use our religion—in this case, Christianity—to make ourselves feel better.

But is that really wrong? I mean, there's enough stuff in the world to make us feel bad. Between disease, poverty, political injustice, and all the other everyday problems of life, surely it's not wrong to look to Jesus to feel better.

That's not wrong really. Jesus did say that He came so that His followers would not only have life, but have an incredibly full life—an abundant one. So in a sense, Jesus does make us feel better, but His definition of that is much different than ours. Too often we are guilty of thinking that life with Jesus is somehow supposed to be easier—more comfortable—than life without Him.

I wonder what those twelve disciples who first walked with Him would say about that. Those guys who heard Him first talk about the abundant life that comes along with Him are the same ones who spent their lives undergoing persecution and hardship. Many lived without homes. Eleven were killed for their faith. So how is that life abundant?

You could answer that question in a lot of ways. It's abundant because of the peace of knowing that God is in control. It's abundant because you know your life is about something bigger than yourself. It's abundant because lasting joy can really only be found in God through Christ. It's abundant because with Jesus, there is the promise of another life—an eternal one—that will make this one seem like a hazy dream. And then there's this: Life with Jesus is abundant because it is life lived deeply.

I think we all want that last one. We want to walk deeply with Jesus. That walk is deeply satisfying. It's deeply abundant. It's deeply mysterious in a very good way. The hard part about walking deeply with the Son of God (so I've heard from those who do) is that it's also deeply uncomfortable.

The road to a deep, authentic walk with Christ looks different for everyone, but I think most of those roads have similar characteristics. Many of them involve a season of extreme difficulty usually because of life circumstances. More of them involve a commitment to practicing the classic spiritual disciplines that position us to receive truth from the hand of God. And all of them require an ever-increasing commitment to faith and obedience. But all of these characteristics also have this in common—they are a struggle.

That's what I hope this volume of *Tough Sayings* is for you and me both. I hope it's a chance for us to be discontent with what is comfortable and to struggle with a Jesus who refuses to be domesticated by modern church standards. I hope it creates dialogue about what it really means to walk along life's journey with Christ in a deeper fashion.

It reminds me a little of the fascinatingly bizarre Old Testament story of Jacob, the shifty, deceptive son of Isaac. He spent a night wrestling with an angel of the Lord (or perhaps God, depending on who you talk to). And after that night he was different. He emerged with a new name and a new blessing because he "struggled with God and with men and . . . prevailed" (Genesis 32:28). But he also came out with something else: a limp. His walk was changed forever because of those moments he spent grappling with the Lord.

Maybe the same thing can happen to us. Wrestling isn't easy; it's certainly not comfortable. And we will be marked because of having done it. We will walk differently than we did before. But that struggle is part of a walk with Jesus who is not defined by comfort and ease; it's defined by the unsafe, unconventional, controversial Son of God.

Read on. Question. Process. Wrestle. And hopefully limp.

We want to walk deeply with Jesus. That walk is deeply satisfying. It's deeply abundant. It's deeply mysterious in a very good way. The hard part about walking deeply with the Son of God is that it's also deeply uncomfortable . . .

Read on. Question. Process. Wrestle. And hopefully limp.

"AND I TELL YOU, MAKE FRIENDS BY MEANS OF THE UNRIGHTEOUS MONEY . . ."

SESSION 1

FRIENDS WITH MONEY

Movies are very different than they used to be. I'm no film critic and I haven't been going to the theater for that long in the grand scheme of cinematography, but even in my limited experience and expertise, I've noticed an interesting development. In years past it was clear who we, as part of the audience, were expected to root for. Whether it was Superman, Indiana Jones, or Luke Skywalker, we knew who the hero was, and so we also knew whose side we should be on. But now things are different.

The current trend is toward no real hero—at least not in the square jaw-line, unquestionably brave, ever-moral sense. Instead, we find ambiguous sorts of protagonists who are simply people we bear witness to. We sort of root for them, but we are also exposed to their failings. Even if they're "good," they often have the same shortcomings that the villains used to have, and consequently we are meant to be onlookers to a story rather than people pulling for someone in a clear-cut account of good and evil. And while we may expect to find this non-hero approach in the evolving entertainment industry of the "blurring-the-lines" kind of world we live in, we do not expect to find ambiguity in the parables of Christ.

For a first-hand look at this kind of movie-making, compare a classic superhero movie with a biopic. For example, watch the original *Superman*, then watch *Walk the Line*. Notice the differences in how the protagonist is portrayed.

THE ANTI-HERO

Jesus' teachings, of all things, should offer us a moral center, a compass to show us the right direction. The characters in His stories should be straightforward and faithful, holding true to the ideals that all of us aspire to. We might sit in a movie theater and wonder who the good guy or bad guy is, but we certainly don't expect that from Jesus. Not in His stories. There the issue is clear: The Good Samaritan is the good guy (Luke 10:30-35). The shepherd is the good guy (Luke 15:1-7). The waiting father is the good guy (Luke 15:11-32). Simple. Straightforward. No ambiguity. Until we get to Luke 16, that is. There we're confronted with a moral dilemma that leaves us asking, "So who am I supposed to root for?"

Read Luke 16:1-13.
Who would you say is the good guy? The bad guy?
Why do you say that?

Which parts of this parable seem strange to you?

CAUGHT RED-HANDED

This particular parable begins with an introduction of the two main characters. There is the rich man, and there is the guy who has been placed in charge of the rich man's stuff. As a manager, or steward, he was in charge of caring for the affairs of his employer. The language of the passage suggests that the steward had been in such a position for a while and that he had grown accustomed to his privileged "white collar" status. He liked the ease of his existence and had no doubt carved out a pretty comfortable lifestyle for himself. That made his problem all the more acute.

The problem was that people were talking, and they were talking about him. But they weren't just spreading idle rumors; the gossip around town had some serious teeth to it. Apparently this guy's work ethics, lifestyle, and overall attitude hadn't won him any friends. The charges swirling about him and his work came with hostile intent, and people were going to the boss with stories of gross misuse and mismanagement of funds. What made matters worse for the steward was that the owner had no trouble believing the accusations. So he didn't nonchalantly stroll over to the steward and ask if the rumors were true. Nope, the master had already made up his mind. He demanded an answer and informed the slacker that he would be fired.

What was the steward to do? He had his lifestyle, his comfort, and his status to think about. He was not about to take a hit to his pride and lower himself to the point of begging or doing some kind of manual labor. He was surely far above that. In order to keep his pride—and luxury—in tact, he needed a way out of this predicament.

But what could he do? His fate was sealed, so it would do little good to throw himself at the mercy of his boss. He obviously had a bad reputation since the townspeople were responsible for tattling on him in the first place. Can you see the shifty steward in your imagination? Maybe he was a little overweight because of his cushy lifestyle. Picture him pacing the floor of his workspace, sweating both with the heat of the day and his growing anxiety. Squirmy, wiggly, shifty—the steward racked his brain.

Then suddenly, a clever smile lit across his face. He had found a way out. With his options dwindling, he took hold of the only thing he had left in his control: his master's books. The financial records, at least temporarily, were still in his care.

> If the parable ended now, what emotion would you feel toward the steward? Toward the master?

The word *steward* comes from the combination of the Greek words for "house" and "administer." A steward in this time was one who manages the domestic affairs of a family or a minor. It's applied in Scripture to managers of assets but also to apostles and ministers of the gospel (1 Corinthians 4:1; Titus 1:7-9).[1]

In referring to the rumors about the steward, the word used is *diaballo*, which means, "to bring charges with hostile intent." The intent of the word is so hostile that this verb shares the same root as *diabolos*, "the devil."

If the parable ended now, what point would you expect Jesus to make? Why?

The manager ran—at least as fast as his heavy, well-fed frame would carry him—to the desk and opened those volumes of names and numbers of people who had borrowed money from his master. He scanned the lines until he at last found what he was looking for. Then he prepared himself to make a couple of community visits.

The steward picked out two good people to call on, for both of the debtors he chose owed a large sum of money. The first owed his debt in the form of oil. According to the text, "a hundred measures" were required of him (v. 6). One measure of oil is roughly equivalent to 8.75 gallons, making his debt about 875 gallons of oil or the yield of about 150 olive trees. Put in the terms of the day, it would take an average laborer three years to pay off this debt if he put every last penny of his salary toward it. The second debtor was in a similar situation except with wheat. He owed "a hundred measures of wheat" (v. 7), which is about 1,100 bushels. If the same daily laborer wanted to pay off this debt using all of his salary, it would take him somewhere between eight and ten years. These were not piddly amounts or handshake loans from a friend; they were significant, and the manager was going to take full advantage of each situation.

SHREWD MOVE?

You can imagine the excitement of the two debtors when the steward told them that he was lowering their debt—by a lot. To the first he required only half of the hundred measures; to the second he took the debt from one hundred to eighty bushels, literally knocking years off their balance sheets. Obviously this guy's hope was to make a few friends while he still had some leverage so that when he was inevitably tossed out onto the street, a few people at least would be willing to give him a chance at a job. Remarkably in the end, though, the master praised the unrighteous manager because of his shrewdness. Likewise, Jesus then said that we should take a lesson from the steward.

Oil was an indispensable commodity in the ancient world. Besides being used as food, fuel for lamps, medicine, cosmetics, and in religious ceremonies, it was also used as a means of trade. Oil was kept in the royal storehouses alongside of gold, silver, and spices, and even used as a means of paying taxes to rulers.[2]

What questions do Jesus' response bring to mind?

How does this parable fit with what you know about the character of Jesus? How does it seem to contradict it?

Are you kidding? Surely Jesus got this wrong. Maybe what He meant to say was, "Blessed are you when you do not act like the shady steward." After all, here was a man who was, at worst, a thief skimming off the top of his employer's books and taking more than he should or, at best, a worthless and lazy business manager who didn't take care of what had been entrusted to him. Then to make matters even worse, rather than owning up to his mistakes, he went behind his master's back in yet another sneaky move that cost his boss a ridiculous amount of money. The quality that spawned this kind of half-hearted work and crafty deceit is not one that I'd consider exactly worthy of pursuit.

And frankly I expect more from Jesus. After all, isn't He the One always telling me to do better? To act better? To be better? And yet here it seems He is suggesting that it's OK to do worse!

Perhaps we can start to sort out this mess by asking what parts of this steward's actions deserved praise from either the rich owner or Jesus. At first glance it seems both should be offended—the owner for the financial compromise and Jesus for the moral one—yet both slapped him on the back with a surprising "attaboy." Let's consider for a moment, though, just how clever the servant's response was. Put aside any temptation to think, *So he reduced the debts? What's so smart about that? Any idiot would have done the same thing.* Think about all the implications involved in those two simple acts. This was a calculated move with an even slyer reason than simply making friends.

What does the word *shrewd* mean to you?

Does the word *shrewd* have a positive or negative connotation to you?

Do you consider yourself to be shrewd? In what ways?

Shrewd has some negative connotations associated with it. Images of black markets, under-the-table dealings, and questionable tax returns flood our minds. But sometimes we root for the shrewd guy, and not necessarily the good guy. Take *Ocean's Eleven* for example. They're criminals, and shrewd to be sure; but we can't help but root for them. Plan a movie viewing with some friends.

THE REST OF THE STORY

Perhaps the steward's reason was one of vengeance. After all, here was a chance to make friends who might benefit him later and at the same time get back at his master where it hurt most—in the wallet. But maybe the shrewdness ran even deeper than that. The Mosaic Law, the very basis for cultural life in Israel, expressly forbade Jews from charging interest on loans they made to other Jews. Granted, this law was a bit like the speed limit in our culture today—generally regarded as a nice idea but not exactly effective in the real world—so most people fudged on it. And no one talked about how they compromised this area of Jewish ethics. The total of the outstanding debts owed to the master included not only the amount that was borrowed but the interest he was illegally charging on top of that.

It's possible the servant simply removed the interest, and in so doing, moved his master back in line with the Mosaic Law. If this was the case, the real genius of the plan came in the way it manipulated the rich man. Upon hearing that the debt was reduced, if the master reacted harshly, he would become known as the guy in the community with no regard for the law and who exploited people in need of money. The only option for him was to react favorably—to grit his teeth, smile, and congratulate his former employee: "Crafty, steward, very crafty."

Of course, that still does not address the issue of why *Jesus* commended his actions. While the master was forced into commendation, Jesus was not manipulated by anyone. (After all, He was the one making up the story to begin with.) But the Son of God also possesses the unique ability to separate sin from sinner, heart from result, and characteristic from application. Notice that Jesus commended the shrewdness the man displayed—a far cry from commending his unrighteousness application of that shrewdness. Jesus wasn't endorsing vengeance, laziness, or trying to get away with shady behavior. He was, however, commending the cleverness behind those things.

What part of shrewdness do you think Jesus is commending?

In what other ways can we separate the characteristic from the application?

Leviticus 25:36 clearly forbids charging interest on a loan. However, in its context, the prohibition against interest is meant to protect someone who is poor and destitute. God's people were supposed to support and encourage the poor rather than take advantage of them to make a profit. We do not know whether the borrowers in Luke 16 were impoverished and therefore can't say if the lender was in violation of the spirit of the law.

Jesus is not the only one who can draw distinctions like this; we do it all the time. My 3-year-old has become fascinated with Kleenex. Can you blame him? It's a self-replenishing box of fun—pull one out and another immediately appears in its place. The only problem is that Kleenex to Joshua is like white powder to a cocaine addict—he can't pull just one and then marvel at the next one coming. He is obsessed, pulling and whipping and throwing and wasting. One afternoon Joshua found himself in the pleasurable situation of sitting on the floor with a full box of tissue. It didn't take long for the paper to start flying.

Listen to "You Are" by Mark Roach on the *Tough Sayings* playlist. Your leader will send it to you via e-mail, or you can find it at *threadsmedia.com/ media*. How well do you know who Jesus is? When was the last time He surprised you?

I was a casual observer, amused at first, but then I realized I needed to play the parental role and bring some discipline into my son's life. So I approached him with a warning: "Joshua, don't pull another Kleenex," to which he promptly responded by pulling not one but two more fluffy sheets in rapid succession. So I used my best "scare-you-into-obedience" voice and moved in for a sterner statement: "Joshua, if you pull one more Kleenex, you are going to time out."

That made him think. I could see the wheels began to turn as he looked up at me with the eyes of an adrenaline junkie and then down again at the object of his obsession. He considered the matter carefully and for 10 seconds did nothing. Then, at long last, he stood to his feet, looked at me one last time, pulled a Kleenex out of the box, marched with it in his hand to the time-out corner, and sat down.

What are you going to do with that? I felt divided, and the suppressed laughter in my voice betrayed me. I wasn't laughing because his disobedience was funny or even commendable—far from it. However, even though he was obstinately defiant, I had to smile. Though I wasn't proud of his choice, I was proud that he had considered the matter carefully. (I also smiled because it was funny.) I was happy that my son was prepared for the consequences of his actions and, in a sense, was willing to "take it like a man." I instinctively was able to commend the spirit behind his actions—his resolve, decision-making ability, and perseverance—without commending the way that those characteristics worked themselves out.

We draw distinctions in other areas of life too. Regardless of our stance on the current hostilities in the Middle East, for example, none of us would approve of a suicide bombing or the tactics of terrorism. But can't we appreciate the bravery and resolve of someone willing to give his or her life for a cause, and at the same time, absolutely abhor the end to which that resolve leads? We can appreciate the quality, but hate the avenue in which that quality works itself out. We can, and I think Jesus did.

LOOK AHEAD

It was not the steward's dishonesty that Jesus commended, and it's certainly not dishonesty that Jesus is after in the lives of His followers. It's the shrewdness that led to the dishonesty that Jesus wants us to emulate. Knowing this, however, leads us to a couple of questions: What exactly does it mean to be shrewd? And what is the proper outworking of that characteristic in the life of someone who follows Jesus?

Are there certain areas of life in which Christ-followers should be shrewd and certain areas in which they should not? Why?

When I think about someone who is shrewd, my mind immediately creates an image of an individual who has greasy hair, a malevolent laugh, and a long, thin mustache that he rolls in his fingertips. It's a characteristic of those who get away with stuff they're not supposed to get away with. They may not be dishonest, but they're certainly not on the up and up. They're shady. They're smarmy. They're a hair above the law, but they tiptoe back and forth across that line. Yet my definition of shrewdness is once again colored by my inability to separate the characteristic from the potential evil outworking of that characteristic. In reality, to be shrewd means little more than using practical wisdom or common sense. Think of it as street smarts. It's taking advantage of every opportunity and not walking blindly into any situation. It is, at least in the case of this steward, focusing on the future.

That's something Jesus wants from all His followers: an acute awareness of their future that results in the taking advantage of every single opportunity that presents itself to them. The steward knew that he had a short time of employment left and that he needed to prepare for what was coming next. Likewise, everyone on this planet—whether a follower of Jesus or not—has a relatively short time here. We've been given resources for the duration, and, like the steward, we can look at the "books" of the master we've been given. We can simply enjoy the days we have—allowing life to happen to us—or we can think about the future and do something about what's coming next. We can use our stuff, particularly money, to "make friends" now so that when the money fails someone will be waiting to welcome us into what comes next (v. 9). But what does that really mean? Is Jesus really suggesting that we form our own sort of entourage, a group of paid-for-pals that hangs around as long as the cash keeps flowing?

Shrewd—
Archaic; mischievous. Given to wily and artful ways or dealing.

The steward's actions are translated differently in various versions of the Bible. The HCSB says he acted "astutely." The Message opts for "streetwise." The Contemporary English Version says that the steward was "looking out for himself so well."

What do you think Jesus means by using money to make friends?

Phronimos in Greek, shrewdness is an admirable characteristic in passages like Matthew 7:24; Luke 12:42; and 1 Corinthians 10:15. However, it is also used negatively. In that sense, it is translated "conceited" and "proud" (see Romans 11:25; 12:16).

Read Ephesians 5:15-16.
What do you think it means for the Christ-follower to take advantage of every opportunity?

Verse 9 is an interesting part of the Luke 16 text. Jesus said that the money will fail, but "they" will welcome us into eternal dwellings. "They" are the people we have made our friends on this earth through the use of money. Here's another way to put it: "They" are those who have come into the family of God because of our influence on this earth. "They" are the ones who have begun to follow Jesus because we did not choose to just walk through life, but to think about the future. "They" are the Indonesians and Afghans and others who have discovered Jesus because we chose to spend our cash for the sake of the kingdom of God rather than another movie ticket. "They" are the homeless family who got back on their feet because we chose to eat fewer meals at restaurants and give away more money.

"They" are all the people who have been impacted by our shrewdness because we began to see finances as a tool for the kingdom of God rather than a means by which we can make ourselves more comfortable. That's how we are shrewd with our money—we consider the future and put our funds to work for a purpose greater than ourselves.

Who are "they" to you?

What are a few practical ways you can be shrewd with your money to impact others for now and the future?

We might wonder, though, why Jesus cares so much about our money. It seems like it's all about the Benjamins (or Jacksons, as the case may be), and our relationship to them. Apparently Jesus is incredibly concerned about money, and as this passage concludes you see why: "No household slave can be the slave of two masters, since either he will hate one and love the other, or he will be devoted to one and despise the other. You can't be slaves to both God and money" (Luke 16:13).

Why, Jesus? Why do you care so much about my salary? Why do you concern yourself so much with this area of my life? It's because our wallets, maybe more than anything else, are a great indicator of our hearts. Our bank accounts reveal more truly than our words ever will what we really value. They show what we really care about. It's not that you can buy your way into the good graces of God; it is, however, that if you really do care about Jesus and His kingdom then your finances will show it. So you could say that there are two kinds of people in the world—those who are mastered by their money, and those who have mastered their money and can therefore use it as a tool for good.

EASIER SAID THAN DONE

Don't be mastered by your money. It sounds simple, doesn't it? Master your money, and in that mastery use it as a tool for eternity. But it's more complicated than just willing ourselves to do more good with our money. It's more complex than just deciding to not be ruled by money anymore. To get out from under its thumb and to start shrewdly using money as a tool, we have to ask why so many of us are under its rule in the first place. I know that in my own life, I'm not so much under the rule of cash itself but with the things that it can get me. Consequently, though, I still live enslaved by the means that get me that stuff I think I "need."

Logic tells me that if I didn't need all that stuff, then I wouldn't need money to get it. And if I didn't need money, then I'd be able to use it in the way it was intended. So the key question at the end of that trail is this:

In 2000, American evangelicals made $2.66 trillion in income, but giving by North American churchgoers was higher during the Great Depression than in 2004. Thirty-three percent of U.S. born-again Christians say it's impossible for them to get ahead in life because of the debt they carry. Check out *generousgiving.org* for more information.

In Tom and Christine Sine's book *Living on Purpose*, they claim that nearly all of us live reactively rather than proactively. Check out this challenging assessment to start thinking about the way you operate financially so that you can actually do something instead of get something else.

Why do I need all that stuff? Why do I need new clothes and a nice car? Why do I need a case of DVDs and a high-definition TV? Surely the answers are as many as the pieces of unworn clothing that hang in my closet, but in essence they all add up to this: Each thing I use money to buy is an effort to meet a perceived need. I have all these needs swirling around in my mind and heart—the need to be loved, to be liked, to be valued, to be important—and I spend my money on things that ultimately broaden those holes in my soul rather than filling them. The result is always moving from one material item to another, and never having the peace that would surely come if those holes were filled. We are experts at trying to use stuff, self-destructive actions, and relationships to try and "complete" ourselves.

Would you say that you control your stuff or that your stuff controls you? Why?

What "needs" do you use money (or the stuff you buy with it) to fill?

How do you think God feels about the way you use your money?

SHALOM

Peace. That's what it would feel like if we had mastery over our money. We wouldn't feel like we had to have anything. We could take and leave things at will because we were in control. Jesus' audience would have called that experience *shalom*. The word is translated peace, but it actually has a much broader meaning. Shalom is not just the absence of conflict but a way of life. It's greater than the absence of conflict. It describes a life that is complete. Indeed, the fullest meaning of shalom is "wholeness" or "completeness"—and the result is wanting for nothing. Notice that we want for nothing not because we have everything, but because we are already complete. And there we find the key.

In Luke 16, Jesus told a story that had as its point this: We need to use our money as a tool to think about the future. Easier said than done, Jesus, because we need our money. We need it because we do not live in shalom; we do not live in completeness. Or at least we don't think we do.

Fortunately, Jesus had been thinking ahead in Luke 15 where He gave us the key to wholeness. If you scan back a chapter, you'll see that Jesus was telling parables there too. In fact, it's almost as if He started a string of stories in Luke 15 to be extended into Luke 16. The stories in Luke 15 have a very different theme, though. In that chapter, Jesus talked about a sheep, a coin, and a son to illustrate this point: God places incredible value on people. Shown through the picture of a shepherd who leaves ninety-nine to save the one, a woman who goes to extraordinary lengths for a moderately valuable coin, and a father so overcome with love for his son that he humiliates himself to welcome him home, Jesus clearly meant to point out that regardless of what the world says, God values you. He thinks you are important. He likes you.

Read Luke 15.
What other points can you pick out of these parables?

Do you think God really *likes* you? Why or why not?

"Don't worry about anything, but in everything, through prayer and petition with thanksgiving, let your requests be made known to God. And the peace of God, which surpasses every thought, will guard your hearts and your minds in Christ Jesus" *(Philippians 4:6).*

"God likes me." That's an interesting statement with many implication. For an exploration of this statement along with many others, check out *Abba's Child* by Brennan Manning.

God values you, and that fact, friends, brings peace. It brings wholeness. It brings completeness. If God values me, then I am in want for nothing else. I can live in shalom because of Him. It is as if Jesus was saying, "Please understand the value that you have. Now respond by living in the freedom of wholeness. And one way to respond to that is to no longer be ruled by money in an effort to gain the wholeness that you already have. Realize your value, and be free. Be whole. Be complete." There's no need to fill our holes with stuff. There's no need to use money to manipulate friends or gain power. There's no need to work ourselves to death so we can have more than those around us. We can focus on the future.

Shrewdness and the freedom to exercise it for good is not something we can work toward. It's something that we can embrace because of the completeness that Jesus has already brought to a bunch of lost sheep, misplaced coins, and wayward children. We are His, and we are whole.

This week, take a hard look at your finances. Write down everything you spend in a journal. At the end of the week, divide the results into categories like *Generosity*, *Food*, *Bills*, and *Entertainment*. Make some resolutions based on what you find.

Try being intentional about generosity. Carry $10 in ones with you this week in your pocket. Look for several places to give it away.

Jesus loved to talk about money. Spend some time researching what else He said about it. You can start with these passages:

- **MATTHEW 6:1-4**
- **MATTHEW 6:19-34**
- **MATTHEW 25:14-30**
- **MARK 12:41-44**
- **LUKE 6:27-36**
- **LUKE 16:14-15**

NOTES

NOTES

WHEN HE CAME TO IT, HE FOUND NOTHING BUT LEAVES, BECAUSE IT WAS NOT THE SEASON FOR FIGS. HE SAID TO IT, "MAY NO ONE EVER EAT FRUIT FROM YOU AGAIN!"

SESSION 2

FIGS AND FITS

"Have it your way." That's the slogan of Burger King, but it's also an incredibly appropriate way to describe 21st century society. In our culture, we can not only have things our way, we can have them right away. Everything is customized. Everything is right now. And technology makes it even easier to do life our way, right away. You can have a computer your way, right away just as easily as you can have a hamburger. We can multitask our way through the day, essentially squeezing a workout at the gym, a taco on the road, and a few calls and e-mails from a phone into a one-hour period that once was designated as "lunch." We don't stop for anything—and if a person, business, or relationship doesn't exist within our timetable and can't give us what we think we deserve as consumers, then we'll move on.

That word *consumer* pretty much sums it all up. The consumer consumes, and the consumer rules. Because the consumer rules, everything is geared to make sure that the consumer is pleased, and if the consumer is not pleased, then there is a considerable amount of frustration voiced (usually loudly). Those demands extend into areas of life where we really have no right to demand our way, right away.

Every day, one quarter of the U.S. population eats fast food. American children now get about one quarter of their total vegetable servings in the form of potato chips and French fries. The golden arches of McDonald's are now more widely recognized than the Christian cross. For more facts about our obsession with nuggets, wraps, burgers, and tacos, read *Fast Food Nation* by Eric Schlosser.

FAST FOOD NATION

Take the morning commute, for example. You know what it feels like to sit in traffic crawling toward your destination. Your blood pressure rises by the minute, the air seems thicker coming out of the car vents, and even the wrong song on the radio is enough to set you off. We get that way because our sovereign rights as consumers have been violated by this road construction, and suddenly we can't have our commute our way, right away.

That kind of frustration is a daily reality for most of us—even though it contradicts the biblical virtues of patience and "longsuffering." I want my cable installed today! I want my cell phone to work here! I want my hamburger with no onions! In the end we are quick-tempered and are likely to fly off the handle at virtually anything that gets in the way of the agenda we have set for ourselves. I'm not saying it's right; I'm just saying it's the way we are.

Yet, while it may be commonplace for us, it's certainly not an attribute that we expect to find in Jesus.

> Read Mark 11:12-14,20-26.
> What questions does this account raise for you?

> How would you describe the emotional state of Jesus in this passage?

At first glance, this account is troubling indeed—and not just because it doesn't seem to make any sense. It's troubling because of the attitude that we find in Jesus here. We excuse the "my way, right away" attitude

34

in ourselves, chalking it up to societal pressure, but we aren't ready to give Jesus the same benefit of the doubt. We routinely throw our own pity-parties, temper-tantrums, and adult-sized fits—but surely not Jesus. So who is this angry consumer beating up a fruit tree we find in Mark 11? Could it be the Son of God who we like to think is so patient with us?

Of course, Jesus' frustration was certainly not without reason. Since the first meal of the day wasn't eaten until midmorning, Jesus, as well as the disciples, would have been understandably hungry. Add to that the realization that Jesus' time on earth was drawing very close to the end. With the crucifixion looming on the horizon, He had every right to be a little on edge. Still, we expect better. Jesus is supposed to be above things like that. Yet there He was, seemingly exercising His power just because He could—and all because He couldn't have what He wanted, when He wanted it.

UNFAIR EXPECTATIONS

The situation becomes even more complicated when Mark's account of these tense moments tells us that it wasn't even the season for figs yet. We know from the context that this was around the time of Passover, which usually came in April. Apparently leaves are found on Palestinian fig trees except for the three winter months, and ripe figs are present from June through November. Everybody knew that. No reasonable person would expect fruit in April, and certainly Jesus was a reasonable person. Why was He so angry, then?

If we have questions like that, just imagine what the tree must have thought. There he (or she, as the case may be) was, minding his own business, waiting for the right time to produce fruit, when up walks a man along with several others in tow. *But why are they coming? They can't be coming expecting fruit . . . can they? It's not time!* But that's exactly what they're looking for. Unfair! Unjust! Unreasonable! Who does this person think He is, judging me for something that I am incapable of doing?

That perspective sounds a little too familiar to me on two fronts. It's familiar on a personal front because I often feel like Jesus is mad at me for things that I find to be unreasonable. How can I be expected to provide for my family and give to support the poor of my community? How can I be expected to remain patient and faithful when career opportunities don't

The account of the cursing of the fig tree was incredibly close to the crucifixion. Considering Jesus was crucified on a Friday, His encounter with the tree was likely on Monday of the same week.

The fig tree is of symbolic importance throughout Scripture. Again and again it is used by God to indicate the prosperity of the Jewish nation (2 Kings 20:7; Isaiah 38:21). When nurtured, fig trees can grow to be 30 feet tall and can live for more than 400 years. However, in the wild, they straggle uncontrolled over the rocks and stony places. Figs are generally shaped like pears. The actual fig is the container that holds the true fruit of the tree—the small seeds that can be felt in one's mouth when eating a fig.[3]

work out? How can I be expected to remain honest and upright when I deal with a mechanic who isn't? Unreasonable.

In what ways can you identify with the tree?

Have you ever thought Jesus had unreasonable expectations of you? What were the circumstances?

SOME SHEEP AND SOME GOATS

The tree's perspective also sounds familiar because it smacks of another passage in the Bible. The other is a story that Jesus told, and it's found in Matthew 25. Interestingly enough, Jesus spoke this parable within weeks—maybe even days—of when He cursed the tree.

Read Matthew 25:31-46.
Does anything bother you about this story?

What was the separation of the sheep and goats based on?

The New Testament mentions sheep 74 times; only one instance refers to literal sheep. The word is more often used as a metaphor for those who follow God. The reasons Christ-followers are called sheep are numerous: Sheep are defenseless, they are utterly dependent on the shepherd, and they are animals meant to follow rather than lead. All of these are descriptive in terms of a relationship with Jesus.

The story of the sheep and goats finds its place in the middle of Jesus' teaching about the end of the world and the things that will happen then. There are a few parallels to the fig tree—both are agricultural in nature, both deal along the lines of judgment, and both were taught by Jesus during His final few days on earth. But the most striking parallel is the similarity between the sheep, the goats, and the tree when all three encounter the judgment of Jesus.

According to the story, there will be a time in the future when everyone will be gathered before Jesus, and He will separate them into two groups—sheep to the right, goats to the left. For the sheep group, Jesus will have a reward ready for them to inherit. For the goat group, there will be eternal punishment. It's a pretty strict division, and you'd definitely not want to find yourself on the "goat" side. Notice the shocked response of the goats, though. Jesus claimed that they had opportunities to feed Him, give Him something to drink, give Him clothes, and offer Him hospitality, yet they refused. Their response? "Unfair! Unreasonable! We never saw you sick or hungry or thirsty or naked or in prison. How can we be judged for something like that? It's completely unjust."

Sounds a lot like what I imagine the tree would have thought. The question of the tree and the goats is clear: "How can you fault me for something I could not have done?"

Listen to "When I Leave" by JJ Heller on the *Tough Sayings* playlist. Your leader will send it to you via e-mail, or you can find it at *threadsmedia. com/media.*

What's your definition of *fair*?

Has it ever felt like Jesus treated you unfairly? When?

How did you deal with that reality?

FARMER JESUS

So what if it was unfair? Maybe Jesus was a little out of sorts. As we've already said, Jesus had a ton on His mind when He encountered the fig tree. Maybe we just need to cut Him a break. But there's another interesting detail that might shed some light on the situation. Let's not forget that Jesus was a native of Palestine.

He grew up there. He knew about the landscape. For that matter, He had walked it for three years straight with His disciples. I personally have never been to Israel. I couldn't recognize a fig tree from an apple bush. If I were to locate a fig tree—on the off-chance that I did somehow wind up in Israel—I'm sure I'd walk up to a it and still not know what to look for, regardless of the season. But you would expect that someone—like Jesus for example—who had lived in a place for more than three decades would know when it was appropriate to expect a common thing like figs and when it wasn't.

If that's the case—if we give Jesus a little credit for knowing something about life in His culture and the food supply of His region—then things don't add up. Why would He be mad when He knew full well that it wasn't the season for figs? But they start to make a little more sense when we once again look back at the timing of the incident. Remember that this happened in late March or early April, a time of year when there were no figs . . . but there were leaves. Jesus would have seen the leaves from a long way off. And knowing the landscape and agriculture as He did, Jesus would have known that at the same time leaves appear on fig trees, a kind of forerunner also grows there.

It's a pre-fruit, if you will, that grows to the size of an almond and is suitable for eating. These "fig-lets" were often eaten, especially by peasants and those passing by the trees. These pre-fruits, called *taqsh* in Palestinian Arabic, eventually drop off after a few weeks, and the true fig appears about six weeks later. If the leaves appear but the taqsh do not, then that is a strong indication that there will be no figs. Jesus would have known that.[4]

Jesus would have seen the leaves. He would have expected to find these pre-fruits. Jesus approached the tree because there was every indication that it would offer something more than just leaves; He found nothing. No taqsh. Just leaves. So He cursed it, and it died.

Does this information change your thoughts about the story?

If Jesus was using the tree as a teaching tool, what do you think He was trying to teach?

JESUS MAKES A SCENE

OK, so now we know that Jesus was not throwing an unwarranted temper tantrum because the leaves indicated something else would be there. In essence, the leaves lied to Jesus and He got mad. Keep reading the text, though (vv. 15-19), and you'll see that the tree was not the only thing that made Him angry that day.

Leaving the cursed fig tree, Jesus and His disciples went into the temple complex in Jerusalem. The complex was divided into a series of successive courts, each becoming more and more restrictive in terms of who could enter. The incident described in verses 15-19 took place in the outer court, the Court of the Gentiles. That court was supposed to be a place for non-Jews to offer their sacrifices, as well as a place for Jews going further inside to prepare themselves with prayer and meditation. But by the time of Jesus, this ancient outer court was a far cry from the place it was originally intended to be.

All Jews who went to the temple had to pay a yearly tax. They obviously had to bring this with them to the temple, but that became a problem for those who were living in other parts of the world. Since it was Passover, international Israelites would be traveling from their homes to Jerusalem, and because the tax had to be paid in a specific form of currency—shekels of the sanctuary—these Jews had to exchange their foreign money. When they went to change their currency, though, they found there to

The whole temple area covered the top of Mount Zion and was about 30 acres in size. The walls surrounding it were about 1,300 feet in length, or the size of four football fields. There was a wide outer space called the Court of the Gentiles where anyone was welcome. At the inner edge of the court, there was a low wall before the next court—the Court of the Women. Next came the Court of the Israelites. It was here that the offerings were handed from the worshipers to the priests who took them into the inmost court—the Court of the Priests. Inside that court stood the actual building, or temple.[5]

be a charge for the exchange. So the international worshipers came away with only two-thirds of the money they brought with them to pay taxes because the exchange booths kept the other third as a fee.

The corruption didn't stop there either. The sacrificial system of the day demanded that unblemished doves be sacrificed at the temple, and while worshipers could buy doves outside the walls, the "temple inspectors" would usually reject them. Conveniently, temple officials had set up stands in the outer court where those who'd come to worship could purchase a dove that was absolutely, one-hundred-percent guaranteed to be without blemish—sure to pass even the most rigorous sacrificial test. And conveniently for the merchants, these guaranteed birds were marked up at an unbelievable rate. Add it up and you get a huge, money-making racket designed to take advantage of those bringing sacrifices.

This scene is what Jesus saw as He walked into the temple, a place set aside for the worship of His Father. And He was mad.

Try to put yourself in Jesus' place. What do you think was going through His mind?

Does Jesus' extreme reaction surprise you? Why do you think He reacted so violently?

Is there anything that you care about enough to react that passionately?

The Greek term *diaspora*, or "dispersion," refers to the scattering of the Jews beyond the boundaries of Palestine. Beginning with the exile in 722 B.C., increasing numbers of Jews left Palestine either voluntarily or by force. By New Testament times, it's possible that three to five million Jews lived outside of Palestine. However, they maintained ties to the homeland and made frequent pilgrimages back to Jerusalem for religious festivals.

WHAT LIES BENEATH

Tables were turned over. People were thrown out. Insults were shouted. The Son of God was furious. And maybe, just maybe, He got upset for the same reason that He was mad at the tree. Maybe Jesus knew what He would find at the temple that day, so He started His lesson for the disciples a few hours early. And maybe that's why the story of the fig tree in Mark is split into two parts by this account of what happened in the temple. And maybe, just maybe, it all comes down to this: Jesus was—and still is—looking for substance, not flash.

How do you see the fig tree in relation to the scene at the temple?

What "substance" do you think Jesus was looking for at the temple?

"Woe to you, scribes and Pharisees, hypocrites! You are like whitewashed tombs, which appear beautiful on the outside, but inside are full of dead men's bones and every impurity. In the same way, on the outside you seem righteous to people, but inside you are full of hypocrisy and lawlessness" (Matthew 23:27-28).

The tree's leaves were a promise: *If you come close to me, you will find something below the surface.* The leaves were an indication that something real, something sustaining, something nourishing would be found beneath. *Just come closer, and you will see,* they called. But in the end, there was plenty of flash—plenty that looked good on the outside—but no real substance beneath.

The temple made a promise, too, as did the people working there. There was plenty of flash around the time of Passover. Crowds were spilling everywhere, people were focused on being pious and devout, and all were concerned with making sure they had the right religious acts in place for their yearly event. But a closer looked revealed what was beneath the flash. The outer stuff seemed to promise real, deep commitment and love for God. Not just leaves, but fruit. Not just flash, but substance. Yet in the end, there was nothing underneath. Just a bunch of religiosity without much heart, plenty of righteousness without emotion, and a ton of rules kept without any love.

If I'm honest, that's more than a little tough to swallow in my own life because I'm often much more like the fig tree and the temple than I care to admit. There's plenty of flash in my own spiritual life, but comparatively little substance. I pay grand lip service to the kingdom of God but do comparatively little to bring about substantial social change. I write about the importance of Scripture and meditating on it but still struggle with regular Bible reading. I talk in persuasive terms about loving my neighbor but am more comfortable inside with my doors locked in the evenings. I think that's true for all of us, especially if we live in a "religious subculture" where worship experiences are the norm, and the biggest question is which comfortable mega-church we'll attend this week.

Maybe all of us, and even our whole system of Western Christianity, are a little more like the fig tree than we care to admit. The church has its own celebrities, production values, and, well, flash. I fear we've created an entire religious system of fig trees that know the right answers but in the end offer little substance and depth.

It would do us well to take a look at our own lives and the church as a whole to see if there is really anything of substance beneath the leaves. Do our words and worship services look good and promise something sustaining and authentic, only to deliver little more than a good show? If Jesus took a close look at us and our churches, would He be sorely disappointed?

> **What are some areas of "flash" that you see in our culture's version of Christianity?**

> **What does "flash" look like in your own life?**

The word "fruit" is used 215 times in Scripture, 106 in Hebrew, and 63 in Greek. It is used literally, figuratively, and spiritually. In the spiritual sense, the fruit is the evidence of the kind of plant that it grows on. That is to say, the fruit reveals the root.

What do you think "substance" means in your life?

HUMBLE SUBSTANCE

Leaves and figs probably look different for all of us, which makes this a difficult question, but it's worth asking anyway: What does someone of substance look like? There are a lot of answers to that question. People of substance have an inner love for God rather than just flashy words. People of substance have had their faith tested through difficult circumstances and have come out faithful on the other end.

People of substance have examined what they believe intellectually, emotionally, and spiritually, and made it their own rather than just blindly following a religious dogma. People of substance care and truly understand the points of view of other people because they are willing to accept the fact that God loves those people, too. There are lots of characteristics that people of substance share. But there is one other substantive trait that is particularly important for our discussion here: Let's turn back to the sheep and the goats.

The goats were surprised by what Jesus had to say, thinking His judgment was completely unfair, but amazingly enough, so were the sheep. They were the ones receiving eternal reward, but it didn't stop them from expressing their own confusion:

> "Lord, when did we see You hungry and feed You, or thirsty and give You something to drink? When did we see You a stranger and take You in, or without clothes and clothe You? When did we see You sick, or in prison, and visit You?" (Matthew 25:37-39).

This attitude seems to be the hallmark of those with substance. When? How? Who? Think about the father who didn't have enough faith for his son to be healed. He told Jesus, "I do believe! Help my unbelief!" and Jesus responded by restoring his son to wholeness (Mark 9:14-29). Or consider the woman whose daughter was sick, so she admitted her absolute nothingness and dependence on Jesus (Matthew 15:21-28).

Modern Christianity frequently throws around the term "relationship" when describing how believers interact with Jesus. That terminology isn't found in Scripture. Instead, the Bible refers to "walking" with Jesus.

Think about Peter, after he denied Jesus three times, when he admitted that he couldn't love Jesus the way that Jesus deserved to be loved (John 21:15-19). These are three people of great substance who, come to think of it, also had the same attitude as the righteous sheep.

It's an attitude of humility before Jesus, an attitude that recognizes how even the best they have to offer and the best things they do, still fall short of what He deserves. And most amazingly of all, Jesus accepted them. They were the sheep. They were the ones with figgy substance.

They were people of substance not because of their great track record. It wasn't because of their knowledge or experiences. In fact, their pedigree fell short in all those areas. No, their substance was built on this fact: they were much more sure of who Jesus is than who they were. And consequently, they were very confident in Him, even if they were very nervous about themselves. Because of their confidence in Jesus, they were willing to walk with an authentic faith—a faith of substance. That doesn't mean it's a perfect faith—far from it in fact. But it means that they were willing to be strong or be weak, be happy or be sad, be confident or insecure, not because they were supposed to but because they knew themselves and God well enough to be real. And that's just what they were—they were *real* people.

The fig tree represents those of Jesus' day—as well as Christians today— who are very sure of their spirituality. They have no doubt in their lives and know the right answer to every question. They exist without humility, basking in the grandeur of their leaves. But Jesus is looking for something more. He is looking for the humble, the honest, the authentic, and the real. He is looking for those who know that the only thing they are really sure of is Him. Those are the sheep. Those are the figs. And the stuff that comes from that kind of spiritual life is almost effortless.

In what ways do you struggle with authenticity in your own spiritual life?

In his classic work, *The Cost of Discipleship,* Dietrich Bonhoeffer wrote, "When Christ calls a man, He bids Him come and die." The book provides an uncomfortably real look at what it means to follow Christ with substance.

Do you think that our brand of Christianity as a whole helps with authenticity or hurts it? Why?

Is there a way to manufacture substance on your own?

Let's look at the sheep one more time. At first glance, this parable is tough because it seems that Jesus handed out judgment based solely on the good stuff we do. But notice this: Jesus did not divide the people and then call them sheep and goats. He knew the sheep and the goats already, and He divided them accordingly. That makes all the difference because it means that the division was based on who they were rather than what they did.

Sheep behave like sheep; goats behave like goats. That behavior is so much a part of who they are, it's almost effortless. Neither the sheep nor the goats realized they were doing good or doing bad because they were acting according to their nature. They were being real. And the sheep proved by their actions that they were indeed sheep. That is substance. That is more than flash. That is real good coming from a person who is real on the inside. Real people don't manufacture substance in the same way that trees don't manufacture figs. The substance that comes from them results in an inner quality that works itself out. For the Christ-follower, that inner quality is a change in their core that has come from a genuine encounter with Jesus. The fruit coming from that change takes all kinds of forms—love, joy, peace, patience, and others—but it's that inner quality that defines people of substance.

It would be tempting for us to walk away from the fig tree with plenty of questions about ourselves: Am I for real? Do I have more than just spiritual flash in my life? Am I a person of deep roots or shallow experience? Those questions are good, of course, but let's finish our discussion of the passage.

Jesus wants to move us to the core of the issue. In the end, the issue is not necessarily about whether or not a church or an individual is too flashy. In the end, the issue is our faith. That's what brings about the inner quality, and that is what is most important to Jesus in this passage.

Jesus continued in Mark 12 with some incredible statements about faith, and that, as always, is the core issue. What do you believe, or more importantly, who do you believe in? Belief in Jesus is not misplaced. Belief in ourselves to "be religious" is misplaced. Let's be honest—of the two of us, Jesus is a lot more trustworthy.

He's the One who is completely obedient to God. He's the One who had the most authentic substance in His walk with God. He's the One who has the strength to hold us up through life. Long after my ability to have the right answers, speak the right words, or react in the appropriate way in any given situation is gone, Jesus is the same. He is stable. Humble faith, more than anything else, is what unites the sheep, the doubting father, the dejected mother, and the stumbling disciple. In the end, we may be unsure of ourselves, but we can be sure of Jesus. And if our confidence is in Him, then we have the freedom to live in authenticity. In humility. In reality.

And we will know that there are more than leaves in our lives.

- The issue of substance and flash is one that deserves more personal reflection. Take some time in evaluating your own spiritual life. How do you define *substance*? What are the things about you of substance? Journal about your thoughts.

- Spend some time memorizing Jeremiah 17:7-8:

"BLESSED IS THE MAN WHO TRUSTS IN THE LORD,

WHOSE CONFIDENCE INDEED IS THE LORD.

HE WILL BE LIKE A TREE PLANTED BY WATER:

IT SENDS ITS ROOTS OUT TOWARD A STREAM,

IT DOESN'T FEAR WHEN HEAT COMES,

AND ITS FOLIAGE REMAINS GREEN.

IT WILL NOT WORRY IN A YEAR OF DROUGHT

OR CEASE PRODUCING FRUIT."

Ask the Lord to give you deep roots.

- Richard Foster said, "Superficiality is the curse of our age." Pick up a copy of his classic book, *Celebration of Discipline*. Begin to integrate some of his suggestions for living deeply.

NOTES

NOTES

"LAZARUS HAS DIED. I'M GLAD FOR YOU THAT I WASN'T THERE . . ."

SESSION 3

THE WEEPING GENERAL

Value. Now there's an interesting word. You can try and put a dollar amount on value and determine it that way, but in the end, there is a better measure for value than cash. The real test of value is what a person is willing to sacrifice for something. And we're not just talking about money at this point. The fact is, there are few things in our lives that would cause us to sacrifice in order to gain them, keep them, or enhance them. But if we are willing to sacrifice for something, then we can know that it's valuable. At least to us.

And that's sort of the tricky part, isn't it? Since one man's trash is another man's treasure, value seems to be pretty subjective. I may be willing to sacrifice my entertainment budget for a car; you may not. Someone else may be willing to sacrifice his or her late night trips to Taco Bell for a relationship; someone else may not. Someone may be willing to sacrifice all the community they have established in a city for a career opportunity cross-country; another person may not.

VALUE

From these perspectives, it seems as though value is determined by an individual's priorities. Of course, we'd all have to admit that most of us have priorities that are at least a little misplaced, and that makes the question of value difficult. If value is subjective—and we all have messed-up value systems—then is anything universally valuable regardless of the culture, mind-set, or background of the person regarding it?

Which things do you value most?

What is something you think should be of value to everyone?

What do you consider the most valuable thing in the universe?

The most expensive coffee in the world comes from Indonesia and costs about $600 a pound for the beans. Meanwhile, the most expensive chess set in the world sold for $500,000. The most expensive M&M sold for $1,500 becaue it went into space with Buzz Aldrin. For the values of other interesting items, check out *most-expensive.net.*

Continuing on this track, if one person did have absolutely correct priorities, then that person should value what is most precious in the universe. That's where we look to Jesus. Regardless of what you believe about Jesus—whether He's a great teacher or a humanitarian or the One and Only Son of God—I think most of us would acknowledge that He knew how to keep His life in order, to put first things first. So what does Jesus value?

What would you say is the most important thing to Jesus?

What evidence do you find in His life to support that value system?

Unfortunately, this is also a spot where it gets a little sticky because Jesus (once again) has a surprise in store. There are many things we know that

Jesus values: people, tradition, prayer, devotion, cultural relevance, social action, family, Scripture, and the list goes on. We are pretty much OK with those things, but there is a troubling story in the Book of John that threatens to flip our assumptions upside down.

> Read John 11:1-37.
> Is there anything in this passage that bothers you about Jesus' actions?

> What reason does Jesus give for His actions?

Before we get to the happy ending of this story, we have to grapple with the tough details for a while. Jesus had surface-level relationships with hundreds, even thousands, of people. These were the ones who listened to Him teach, supported His ministry, and maybe even became the recipients of His healing. But not the people in this passage. This family was different.

A JESUS WHO WAITS

These people—Mary, Martha, and Lazarus—were much closer than acquaintances. Whenever Jesus went through the region of Bethany He made time for this sister/sister/brother trio. He ate with them. He talked with them. He laughed with them. These people were like His family.

We see it from the text. The message didn't say, "Hey, Jesus, that guy you met that one time on a hillside somewhere, remember him? Well, he's sick." No, it was much more explicit than that. "Lord, the one you love is sick. The person you've sat around a table with and shared intimate moments with needs you." These were not some faceless members of the masses; they were friends-turned-family.

So what did Jesus do about this situation with His good friend? The answer comes across like a slap to the face. He did . . . nothing. Oh, He was quick

The Book of John is not the only place you find a "waiting" Jesus. For another example, spend some time in Matthew 8:23-27.

to make grand statements: "This sickness will not end in death" (v. 4). But then He waited. He stopped. He became stationary. And He did so not only with His feet, but with His being. We know that Jesus didn't even have to go to Bethany to heal Lazarus—just a snap of the fingers, and the disease could have vanished. But He didn't use His power. Not even for the family He loved.

Frankly, that disturbs me. It's disturbing because countless times every day we pray and ask Jesus for action. We want Him to move, to work, to engage. We want Him to change things in our families, our communities, our world, and our lives. And we assume that He is getting our message loud and clear—just like He got this one. And then nothing happens. The cancer gets worse. The job doesn't change. The war goes on.

Meanwhile, we operate with a sense of apprehension in our prayer life. We want to believe that Jesus will come, that He will act, but we have also experienced disappointment in the past. So we put the catch-all phrase at the end of our prayers: "If it's Your will . . . " I think we use that phrase more often to protect ourselves from getting our hopes up again rather than as an acknowledgment of our faith in God's plan.

So what do we do with a waiting Jesus?

When have you felt like Jesus was waiting to act?

How did you deal with that?

The disciples, for their part, must have applauded the waiting, not because they necessarily valued the same thing as Jesus in doing it, but because they were afraid. Bethany was, after all, a growing hotbed of opposition against Jesus. It wasn't long ago that the people there had made serious efforts to kill Him (v. 8). So maybe it only made sense that He would stay put—it was too dangerous, and if Lazarus had to die to protect Jesus, then so be it.

Jesus never had to be present with a person to heal them. In Matthew 8:5-13 Jesus proved His ability to heal anyone, anywhere, at any time.

MORE IMPORTANTLY

Here is where we begin to see the value system of the Son of God come into play. We can only conclude from Jesus' lack of action that there was something more important, more precious, and more valuable than His friend Lazarus. But what was that thing? What could possibly trump the value of relationship, the compassion, and the need for action? Was it the same fear of the region that held the disciples at bay, or was it something else entirely?

Jesus was no coward. He was on His own death march to Jerusalem, and He knew it. No, it was not fear that motivated Jesus' decision to stay. Jesus revealed His reasoning in verse 4: "This sickness ... is for the glory of God, so that the Son of God may be glorified through it."

And there it is.

What do you think Jesus meant by "the glory of God"?

Why is God's glory so important to Jesus?

What makes it difficult to embrace that value system in real-world experience?

The glory of God. That's the motivation. That's the thing of value. That's the thing that trumped Lazarus' sickness and Jesus' desire to help. Here we see God (if indeed you believe that Jesus is at once God's Son and God Himself) acting in the best interests of ... well, God. And we can then answer the question of value: The glory of God—His reputation, fame, and praise—is the most precious thing in the universe. And the thing that Jesus values more than anything else is God.

If you feel like God has let you down, you're not alone. Check out *Jaded* by Mike Harder, another study by Threads, for a more in depth discussion on this issue.

The place of God's glory in the universe is a subject that deserves more attention. Dr. John Piper has made the glory of God his life message. Consider listening to Dr. Piper lecture at *desiringgod.org*.

"The glory of God" is most simply understood as the external manifestation of His being. It is the recognition of who God is, and therefore, God's fame or His renown. The glory of God is shown visibly in Exodus 16:10, but it is also revealed in things like thunderstorms (Psalm 29:4), miracles (Numbers 14:22), and even Christ-followers (2 Corinthians 3:18). Believers don't add to the glory of God; rather, they merely recognize, acknowledge, and display it to others through their lives.

I'll say it again: The thing that God values more than anything else in the universe is God. That may be a hard thing to swallow, mainly because we don't like people who value themselves over anything else. Each of us at one time or another has known someone who seemed to act always in his or her own best interest, regardless of the consequences. We use words like selfish, arrogant, and prideful to describe that person. But it's different with God.

All humans who act consistently in their own self-interest are essentially liars. They lie because in the end they are valuing something that is, in essence, not supremely valuable. The truth is that they are not nearly as great as they think they are. The difference is that God really is that good. He really is that powerful. He really is that loving, holy, and all the other attributes we use to describe Him. All of those things added together make up a God who is absolutely flawless. Perfect. Pristine. Now take it one step further. If God is perfect, then that perfection runs throughout His Being, even into what He values. And if His perfection bleeds into His values, then He must have a perfect value system. And in the perfect value system, God has as His highest value only the thing that is supremely valuable. That thing that is supremely valuable in the universe is Himself.

To take it even further, if God did value something more than He values Himself, He would be a liar, too, because He would then be putting value on something that was not ultimately worthy of it. God's perfection demands that He value Himself above all things.

Or think of it this way: What do we call something in our lives that we love more than God? We call that thing an idol, and we are wrong for putting our love toward it because that thing, regardless of how good it is, does not deserve it. Then it stands to reason that if God gave first place in His life to anything except Himself, then He would become an idolater. Then He would cease to be perfect. Then He would cease to be God.

It's not that Jesus doesn't value those things we talked about earlier—like prayer, devotion, passion, and justice. He does, yet He values them in their proper place. And that place is in relationship to God Himself.

Think of it like a wagon wheel. A wagon wheel has many spokes leading out from a center hub to the edge. Those spokes are important, but they don't hold the wheel together. The hub is what's holding the whole thing in place; it's what is central. In God's value system, those spokes have names on them like, people, family, Scripture, and everything else that is good. But the name on the hub at the middle of the wheel is God Himself. God, in His perfect value system, values that which is supremely valuable, and that's why Jesus waited—because of the glory of God.

> Is there anything that keeps you from accepting this idea?

> What questions does Jesus' decision raise?

> What place does the glory of God hold in your own life?

God's glory dominates His values. Check out a few verses for more information:

- Exodus 20:3-5
- Numbers 14:21
- 2 Samuel 7:23
- Psalm 25:11
- Psalm 106:6-8
- Isaiah 43:7
- Isaiah 48:9-11
- Ezekiel 20:5-9
- Romans 4:20-21
- John 12:27-28
- John 17:24
- Revelation 21:23

CONSEQUENCES

Even if we can accept Jesus' reason for waiting, we still have to deal with the troubling implications in this story. We can acknowledge the importance of the glory of God, but what about the consequences? What about Lazarus? And for that matter, what about all the times in our own lives when Jesus waits? I value the glory of God, and I even understand that it's the most important thing in any given situation, but what about my family? What about my job? What about my health or my dreams or my future? And while we're at it, what about the health and dreams and future of the millions dying of AIDS in Africa or the young girls who are victims of human trafficking? What about the tsunami and hurricane victims? What about the refugee camps?

There are consequences when Jesus does nothing. God may eventually be glorified in every situation, but in this case Lazarus was dying while Jesus waited. And waited. And then waited some more. When at last He made His way to Bethany, Lazarus had been in the tomb for four days. That's significant because it left no doubt about the fate of Lazarus.

Medical technology in the first century was obviously not what it is today. For that reason, it was not extremely uncommon for people to be pronounced dead only to wake up from some kind of comatose state. In fact, after someone was assumed to be dead, people would examine the body, even going out to the cemetery to do so, up to three days after death, just to make sure. John's note that Lazarus had been in the tomb four days indicates that there was no doubt about whether Lazarus was really gone. He was dead. Absolutely.

The time frame also means that the sisters would have given up hope. They had moved past any shred of optimism they were clinging to and into their grief. When Jesus waited, He not only ensured a certain death for Lazarus, but He ensured that Mary and Martha would have begun sitting *shi'vah*, the prescribed seven-day grieving process for any who have lost someone in their immediate family. All the grief, all the pain of the disease, and all the aftermath were ensured by a Jesus who waited.

What do you think was going through the sisters' minds as Jesus waited?

Do you think it was difficult for Jesus to wait? Why?

Besides the lack of medical technology, Jewish folklore played a role in the significance of Jesus' waiting period. The common belief was that at death, the soul would return to the body for up to four days, each time checking to see if the body could receive it back. After the fourth day, the body would have begun to decompose and the soul would move on, leaving no hope for revival.[6]

THE GENERAL

Maybe this idea is so uncomfortable because the picture of a waiting Jesus radically contradicts the very comfortable picture we have of Him in our minds. In that caricature of Himself, Jesus loves us more than anything else in the universe. He would drop everything instantly when someone He loves—like you or me or Lazarus—needed something from Him. He is a little like a butler in that sense—albeit a very loving butler, but someone who lives to take care of our needs.

But the Jesus we see here is not like a butler at all. He's more like a general. During days of war, officers make incredibly difficult decisions every hour of every day. Many if not all of those decisions put good men and women in harm's way. The generals know this. They have to. And yet they make those choices anyway.

They make the tough choices that will inevitably result in loss, pain, grief, and casualties because in order for them to be an effective leader, they have to keep the overall goal in mind. They have to care more about the cause, and make their decisions based on that.

Such is the case with the General of John 11. Like any good general, Jesus knows that the ultimate goal is the most important thing. That goal is the glory of God, and if Jesus is the General, then the war He is fighting is over the glory of the universe. And this General seems willing to make the hard choices, knowing that sacrifices must be made for victory. Lives must be lost. Tears must be shed. Sisters must be disappointed.

All of those things happened in Bethany, but then there was a happy ending. The rest of the story reveals that Jesus did finally go, and His ultimate goal of glorifying God was achieved when He called Lazarus out of the grave. The Jews who had come to comfort the family in their loss saw the power of the Father. God was glorified, Lazarus rose from the dead, and Jesus lived to continue on to Jerusalem.

Still, despite the achievement of that goal, there is a question that wells up inside of us. It nags at us especially during times of suffering. Many times the question is so difficult that it's pushed aside by those who want so badly to honor God with their lives. But every once in a while the question becomes too much, and so it must be voiced. We too may want to be committed to that which is truly valuable, yet in our guts, we can't help but ask, "What about my brother?" or "What about my mom?" or "What about my life?" We know the glory of God is important, but what about the casualties?

At what times do you have questions like that?

The word *shiv'ah* means "seven" and refers to the Jewish custom of sitting in mourning for seven days following the death of a deceased parent, spouse, sibling, or child. It's derived from the account of Job's friends coming to comfort him by sitting silently with him for seven days (Job 2:13). The Orthodox Jewish mourner sits unshod on the floor or on a low stool in the home of the deceased or his near relative. The mourner abstains from all ordinary work and diversions and even from required synagogue prayers, while friends visit him to comfort and pray with him.[7]

In the Book of John, Jesus' miracles are referred to as "signs" because they revealed something not previously known, specifically the fact that Jesus is God. This incident was the final and climactic sign in the book. It was so powerful that it finally pushed those planning the assassination of Christ past the tipping point.

C.S. Lewis' account of the death of his wife, *A Grief Observed*, remains the classic Christian treatment regarding loss. If you haven't explored it, consider making some time to do so.

Why is it difficult to ask hard questions of God?

How do you think God feels about those questions?

FINALLY

I can almost see it in my mind. Jesus gathered up His followers, some of them shrugging their shoulders in disbelief that they were actually going to Bethany after four long days. *What was the use?* they must have thought. As they got to the outskirts of the town, someone came to meet them. Ever the one for action, Martha left her house (and the dramatic grieving process going on there) to meet Him. Also one to shoot straight, she had a question on her heart and mind, so she fired it at Jesus. "What about my brother?" she asked. Yet even as she formed the words, the very sight of the Son of God rekindled the slightest bit of hope: "Even now I know that whatever You ask from God, God will give You" (v. 22).

But Jesus did nothing for her optimism, at least not in her mind. He reminded her of who He was—that He is the resurrection and the life— which she took to mean that someday Lazarus would rise again, along with all the rest of the dead. Then Jesus asked to see the other sister, Mary.

Mary was different from Martha. There is another account in Scripture of Jesus' interactions with this family, and it reveals the starkly different personalities of the sisters. Luke 10 contains the story of when Jesus was staying at their house. Martha was busy while Jesus taught—straightening, cooking, cleaning, preparing. It's no wonder she was ready to get out of the house and run to meet Jesus—she was a doer by nature. But Mary was different. She spent the day that seemed like a distant memory sitting at Jesus' feet as He taught. She listened. She considered. She reflected.

Mary was a thinker. And over the week of her brother's death, she had plenty of time to think and plenty to think about. I'm sure she battled with her thoughts, trying to think and believe the right thing. Her internal dialogue may have gone something like this: *I know Jesus has a reason. I know He loves us. But I also know that He could have healed my brother. So there must have been a very good reason why He didn't come. But what about Lazarus? What could be so important to keep Jesus from being here?* Mary had plenty of time to try and piece things together, but in the end, no matter how much she tried to comfort herself with all the right "church" answers, the question was too much.

Haven't we all had that experience? It's the moment when all the things we have read in the Bible collide full-force with the circumstances of pain in our lives. We know that God ultimately acts in our best interests. We know that He has a plan. We believe He is in control. Yet we also know the pain of loss, grief, and disappointment. And for thinkers like Mary, there comes a moment when theology seems to fail and that nagging question bubbles to the surface.

How do you tend to respond in times of crisis?

How would you describe the way you've tried to handle your own pain in the past?

How do you think God wants you to respond to pain?

In Luke 10:38-42, Jesus stayed at the home of Mary and Martha. In this account, the sisters' revealed their personalities in their different reactions to Jesus. Martha was busy making preparations and doing the chores required with company, but Mary sat quietly and listened at Jesus' feet. Jesus commended Mary for choosing what was better.

So when Martha returned to tell Mary that Jesus had indeed finally come and was asking for her, she agreed to come out. *Come out?* she must have thought. *Of course I'll come out. I need answers.* And so she went—immediately. She raised herself up, fighting back tears of anger, and walked out the front door with such resolve that a crowd followed her there. She walked into the sunlight to see the face of Jesus across the dirt yard. She paused at the sight of Him, but then regained her composure and walked until she was nose to nose with the One who she thought was their friend.

Mary had thought about her question for days, and now it was time to ask. She wanted to put her finger in His face and say all the things in her heart. Then all her boldness and bravery suddenly collapsed, and she fell at His feet in a heap of tears. Through desperate sobs Mary looked up and finally gave voice to her doubts and fears: "Why did you not come? If you had been here, my brother would not have died . . . What about my brother?"

> **What do you think Jesus must have been thinking as Mary questioned Him?**

> **Have you ever had a "Mary moment"?**

> **What are some doubts that you have trouble voicing?**

> **Why is it difficult to voice doubts to God?**

Other translations of John 11:33 say that Jesus was:
- "angry" (HCSB)
- "deeply moved in spirit" (NASB)
- "terribly upset" (CEV)
- "deeply angry" (The Message)

RAGE

We know the cause is important. We know the war is all encompassing, and we know that God's glory is seen through our circumstances, painful though they may be. We also want to embrace the glory for the sake of what is most important, but we understand Mary's question too. It surfaces when the fact that all things work together for good just doesn't seem to be enough (Romans 8:28). It comes to the forefront when you grapple with reality even if you know theologically that in some mysterious way God will be glorified through bad times. This cancer is somehow for God's glory. This car accident is somehow for God's glory. This job loss is somehow for God's glory. But it doesn't make sense in the moment.

The question is uttered when we know that this persecution falling on the house church movement of China is somehow for God's glory. It is expressed when the Indonesian Jihad's taking the lives of believers somehow becomes for God's glory. It is the question we ask when we know that all things will eventually bring glory to God, but still we want to know: What about my brother? What about my mom? What about my friend? What about my people? And what about people halfway around the world?

How would Jesus respond to this question? As Mary collapsed at Jesus' feet, He was deeply moved in spirit and troubled. At least that's what some biblical translations say. Other translations use stronger wording. Many record that sadness was not the only emotion that Jesus felt; they indicate that He felt anger—and not just any anger. Verse 33 carries a sense of especially strong anger, even indignation and rage.

How does your Bible translate the emotions of Jesus in this passage?

What are possible explanations for Jesus' anger?

Why was Jesus angry? Maybe He was mad at Mary. Who was she, after all, to question what He did or did not do? Didn't she understand that He had a mission, and that meant hard decisions? In fact, wasn't she calling into question the very value of the kingdom of God? Besides, in about five minutes He was going to turn the funeral into a party—but there she was, crying on the ground. Pathetic.

One strand of theology known as "The Prosperity Gospel," claims that the result of faith is health, wealth, and a problem free life. According to that ideology, those with strong enough faith will never suffer sickness, financial trouble, or emotional turmoil. Mary, Martha, Job, and the martyred disciples might beg to differ.

TEARS IN THE DIRT

I don't buy that. I don't think Jesus was mad at the grieving sister, mainly because He wasn't just angry—He was also moved. Deeply. Profoundly. Maybe Jesus was angry not because Mary was sad, but because she had to be sad.

Jesus understands better than we do that many times the most effective way for the glory of God to be advanced is through the suffering of His people. He knows that it's one thing for someone to say, "I just got bumped up to a six-figure income, bought a house in the burbs, and have a beautiful wife and 2.5 healthy children. Glory to God!" God should receive glory for all good things in our lives, but it's an entirely different matter when people are weeping over the state of their marriages, their health, and their world—yet they say along with Job in the Old Testament, "I know that my Redeemer lives" (Job 19:25, NASB). That's powerful. That is the evidence of someone who doesn't just stick with Jesus during the good times. And that kind of person propels and magnifies the glory of God . . . even through their pain. That's at least part of the good that can come from suffering; it proves to a doubting world that Jesus is good enough to hang onto.

How have you seen God's glory revealed through the pain of His people?

How do you think Jesus feels about God's glory being revealed through pain?

Jesus knows that suffering is an incredibly powerful avenue for God's glory to go out. He knows it, but He doesn't have to like it. I think that's why He was angry. And I think that's why, as we see in verse 35, He wept. In His tears, you can almost hear His explanation: "I am so sorry that it has to be this way. I am sorry that this war has casualties. And I am sorry for your pain."

Jesus offered no explanation for His action, however, and that is especially meaningful to me. Even though we can read into His reasoning and gain insight into His emotion, He makes no effort to justify Himself. He doesn't bother to give Mary a lesson on the importance of sacrifice for the sake of God. He doesn't launch into a theological treatise about what is really important in the universe. And He doesn't make some pithy statement about how everything will be OK in heaven someday. He simply weeps.

We as Christ-followers can learn something from Jesus' reaction. When tragedy strikes us, people we love, or our community, we're often quick to offer trite clichés and Hallmark-worthy Bible verses: "Don't worry; he's in a better place with no more tears. God works all things for good. Have faith and be happy." Yet Jesus does none of that.

He weeps with people. And that's all.

That part may be even more miraculous than what happens at the end of the account. Think about it: Which is more amazing—a God who can raise the dead or a God, who knows He's about to raise the dead yet chooses to emotionally invest Himself in the pain of His people anyway?

GENERAL IMMANUEL

Here is the General we follow. He is not one who simply barks orders onto the battlefield of life, telling us to attack here and pull back there with His chief concern being whether or not His "troops" follow His directives with unquestioning obedience. Instead, He's the first One into battle and the last One off the field. He's the leader who suffers with His troops.

Somehow, mysteriously, when we find ourselves wounded on life's battlefield, He is there. When our leg catches shrapnel, we look up and see that our General's leg is damaged as well. When the sting of a bullet rips into our arm, we look to our General and see that He has been shot there too. And when our buddy who has been with us through basic training is suddenly gone, and we weep uncontrollably for the loss, we look to our General and see that His tears are bigger than our own.

The Christ we follow knows the full range of human experience. He is not an isolated commander, but one intimately acquainted with the pain of life in the war. He is General Immanuel—God with us. We may rest assured that whatever situation we find ourselves in, God is emotionally involved

Immanuel is a Hebrew word meaning "God with us" and expresses the wonder of God's presence as seen in Jesus Christ. The angel told Joseph in a dream that his fiancée Mary would give birth to a son named "Immanuel." Though God's presence was with His people in the Old Testament (Exodus 25:8), the personal, physical appearance of Jesus—and therefore God's personal, physical presence—far surpassed it.

there too. When we weep at the death of a loved one, our Jesus weeps as well. When we rejoice because all is well, His shouts of joy eclipse our own. And when we fall in the dirt before Him— so sure of theological facts, yet emotionally destroyed by the circumstances of this sinful world—He falls down and weeps with us.

How is Jesus' response to pain different than other responses you have experienced?

Is there any situation in your life where you need to feel Jesus weeping with you?

This is our God. This is the God who knew the end before the beginning. He is the One who knew the resurrection before the crucifixion. He is the One who knew the glory before the pain. Because He knows those things, He can make grand promises about the eternal glory that awaits all those who are His. Yet His response to us in the pain of the human condition is not, "Just believe! It will all be over soon. This is nothing compared to what awaits you." Instead, His response is to walk through the pain with us. His response is to offer His abiding presence in the form of the Holy Spirit until the day when the goal is realized and God receives the glory He deserves.

At the end of this war He will still be there with us, but we will be seated together beside the throne of the Father, scarcely able to remember those times when He knelt in the dirt beside us and wept.

But until that time, maybe sometimes what we need more than just another explanation, another cliché, or another promise of heaven . . . is tears. Tears of the One who understands. Tears of the One who empathizes. Tears of the One who doesn't just tell us that everything will be OK in the end, but of the One who feels our pain as deeply as we do.

- The glory of God in the universe is a complex subject that we should all read a little more about. Consider picking up the book *God's Passion for His Glory*. This resource is difficult to pick through, but contains reflections from America's greatest theologian, Jonathan Edwards. It also contains commentary from Dr. John Piper.

- Have you spent any time with your photo albums lately? Flip through one and remember the people from your past. Do those pictures bring up any unresolved issues you have with God? Pray through them.

- Make an effort to connect more deeply with your group. Is there any situation in your life or in theirs in which you need to feel the tears of Jesus? Share the details together.

NOTES

NOTES

"FOR I TELL YOU, UNLESS YOUR RIGHTEOUSNESS SURPASSES THAT OF THE SCRIBES AND PHARISEES, YOU WILL NEVER ENTER THE KINGDOM OF HEAVEN."

SESSION 4

INSIDE OUT

Certain words are more powerful than others. Obviously, a word like *fantastic* is more powerful than a generic word like *good*, but I mean something more by powerful. I mean heavy. I mean weighty. I mean there are certain words whose mere mention conveys something more than just a word. Sometimes it's a feeling, sometimes it's a story, and sometimes it's just a sense of change.

Words like *inoperable* or *malignant*, *outbreak* or *terrorist*, *birth* or *miracle* are world-changing kinds of words. They're words by which you can really divide your life—before the word and after the word. They are words that cause your breath to catch in your lungs because of joy, fear, or excitement. They're words that make you long for the future or the past. They are words that carry such power, such weight, that they turn upside down what you thought was stable in your life. And while there are a host of words like that, we would probably not expect one such word to be *blessed*.

BLESSED ARE . . .

How does our culture seem to define *blessing*?
How is that different from your definition?

What do you think makes a person "blessed"?

What do you think God means when He calls someone blessed?

There's nothing really special or mystical about the word itself. Sure, we want to be blessed—and most of us consider ourselves blessed in one way or another—but it's certainly not a life-changing, foundation-shaking, upside down kind of word. But in a society built around the idea of blessing and being blessed by God, any teaching or statement that questioned the presumptions they held about these issues would certainly be cause for concern. And any teacher who dared to undermine the long-held understanding of blessing would indeed be controversial.

Maybe that's what it was like for the people on a hill one day when Jesus decided to preach what would become the most famous sermon in history. This traveling Teacher, or Rabbi, had been causing quite a stir as He moved throughout Galilee. He was quickly becoming famous not just for His teachings but also because of His miraculous healings. In fact, we read at the end of Matthew 4 that droves of the sickest, poorest, most destitute, and most rejected people were following this Rabbi wherever He went.

Read Matthew 4:23-5:2.
What is the mental picture you have of the crowds who listened to the sermon that day?

Dallas Willard has a fresh and relevant perspective on the Sermon on the Mount. Read more about it in *The Divine Conspiracy.*

These people were not just beaten down by disease and poverty; they were beaten down by cultural assumption. The prevailing idea during that time was this: It's easy to tell if God has blessed someone—just add up his or her material gain. *Blessing* was defined in terms of good health, a pile of possessions, and a comfortable lifestyle.

The Beatitudes of the culture rang out loud and clear: "Blessed are the rich! Blessed are the well fed! Blessed are the comfortable!" But Jesus flipped that perception on its head. He questioned what people had believed their whole lives. Jesus looked out and saw these crowds—the unlovely, the poor, the mourning, the ragamuffins—and said with love in His eyes, "Blessed are the poor in spirit. Blessed are the mourners. Blessed are the meek and the hungry and the thirsty and the persecuted. Blessed are . . . you" (see Matt. 5:3-11).

That's how the Sermon on the Mount starts: with Jesus in His classically controversial way, challenging the assumptions of the religious and letting us all know once again that we don't have it all figured out.

> Scan through Jesus' sermon in Matthew 5, 6, and 7.
> Which particular verses or phrases stand out to you in the
> Sermon on the Mount? Why?

> What assumptions do you have about Jesus?

The term *Beatitude* comes from the Latin word for "blessed"—*beatus*. Because these statements all begin with Jesus saying, "Blessed are . . ." they became known as the Beatitudes.

JUST JESUS

As if calling the ragamuffins blessed weren't enough, Jesus also looked out and saw in this crowd of the ordinary—the working men and women, the ones who lived paycheck to paycheck and had real life problems and struggles—and said to them, "You are the salt of the earth and the light of the world. You are special. You are important" (see v. 13).

Can you hear the whispering start on the hill that day? As the people sat there looking at this different kind of Rabbi and listening to this new kind of teaching, they must have begun to fidget. They probably stared at one another with a look that said, "Are you hearing what I'm hearing? Can you believe this?" Maybe they even started to talk in hushed voices, saying things like, "This is revolutionary. He is redefining everything we thought we knew about God. Hey, maybe we should just throw out everything else—the written law, the verbal law, and the prophets' teachings. Maybe we should just listen to Jesus and forget everything else!"

Their logic made total sense. After all, Jesus was a unique kind of Rabbi. Other teachers of the day would pronounce the school of thought and tutelage they operated under. A rabbi would refer to his teachers almost like his credentials, as if to say, "Here is what my teacher and his teacher said about this issue." But Jesus did something dramatically different. His credentials were not about who He had studied with; they were based on Himself: "You have heard it said . . . But I say to you . . . "

Jesus did not rely on the oral tradition or someone else's authority. He interpreted freely and authoritatively. What mattered was what He said. When you combine His claim to authority with the rumors circulating about His disregard for certain Sabbath rules, it's not a far stretch for people to conclude that the law and the prophets might no longer be relevant. Sometimes I think we forget that the "Bible" of this day didn't have an Old and a New Testament; they had "a" Testament. The first one. The record of the law and the words of the Prophets—that's it. And Jesus was teaching something dramatically different than what they thought it said.

One of the most popular criticisms against Jesus involved His supposed disregard of the Sabbath. It was Jesus' custom to attend the synagogue on the Sabbath (Luke 4:16), but on six different occasions His actions came into direct conflict with Jewish tradition. For further study on Jesus' Sabbath controversy, see Matthew 12:1-8; Mark 2:27-28; 3:1-5; Luke 13:10-17; and John 5:1-18; 9:1-41.

What about you? How do you feel when you read the Old Testament?

Do you see the Old Testament as relevant in your life today? Why?

Why does your attitude about the Old Testament even matter?

We, too, seem to be ready to sort of disregard the left half of our Bibles. And who can blame us? The Old Testament is full of strange stories and stranger commands. We can find tucked inside its pages directions on how to trim beards, where to go to the bathroom, how to handle skin disorders, the significance of mold, and many other things that frankly don't seem to matter at all in our lives today.

Furthermore, isn't the New Testament full of stuff about being free from the curse of the law and no longer being its slave? I think I remember reading that somewhere. In fact, if you stop to think about it, we're asking pretty much the same question as the people who first listened to the Sermon on the Mount: "How does Jesus relate to the religious writings that came before He appeared on the scene? Where does He fit into the story? Does accepting Jesus mean rejecting everything else, or does He somehow continue what has been going on in God's dealings with His people in the past?"

JESUS AND THE LAW

It was as if Jesus heard the hearts of the people, both then and now, in the way that only He could. Understanding their perspective and questions, He responded before they even had a chance to ask:

> "Don't assume that I came to destroy the Law or the Prophets. I did not come to destroy but to fulfill. For I assure you: Until heaven and earth pass away, not the smallest letter or one stroke of a letter will pass from the law until all things are accomplished. Therefore, whoever breaks one of the least of these commandments and teaches people to do so will be called least in the kingdom of heaven. But whoever practices and teaches [these commandments] will be called great in the kingdom of heaven. For I tell you, unless your righteousness surpasses that of the scribes and Pharisees, you will never enter the kingdom of heaven" (Matthew 5:17-20).

In His teaching, Jesus referenced something called "the Law" and "the Prophets." He apparently had both a solid understanding of and a high regard for the Law and the Prophets—what we call the Old Testament. He thought so much of those writings that He referenced the *yud*, the smallest letter of the Hebrew alphabet, which is little more than an apostrophe. He said that not even a *yud*—the smallest stroke of a pen—would be tossed out of the law. Everything written and experienced prior to Christ was all

The "Law" refers to the first five books of the Old Testament, while the "Prophets" include the books of what we today call the Old Testament written by the major and minor prophets. The expression "the Law and the Prophets" is a way of referring to the entire Hebrew Scriptures.

Torah literally translated, means "teaching" or "instruction." It can be used as a summation term of the entire Old Testament. In the Matthew 5 context, the term refers to the first five books of the Bible or the books of Moses.

legit stuff. Jesus said that He did not come to take anything away—not a single stroke or even the least letter from the Law and the Prophets. According to Him, He wasn't really saying anything knew. He was teaching the same thing that the prophets and those who came before Him had been teaching. His message completely agreed with theirs.

And Jesus knew their message well. The kind of Sunday School that you may have been to as a kid was a far cry from religious education in first-century Palestine. In Galilee, the region where Jesus grew up, a boy would have begun his spiritual studies in earnest at the age of 4 or 5. Each community would hire a professional rabbi, or teacher, who would have been responsible for the education of the village. He would begin instructing the 4- and 5-year-olds, focusing on the Torah, or the Law. The young students would be expected to learn to read and write, as well as memorize large portions of Scripture. They would also begin to learn the Mishnah, or the oral interpretations of the law. Most students had the entire Torah memorized by the time they reached the age of 13, when this level of education would conclude.

At this point only the absolute top students would continue on to a secondary school, studying while they also learned a trade (maybe carpentry, for instance). There, teens would study the Law, the writings of the prophets, and the Mishnah; they would also begin to learn to make their own applications and interpretations. All of this effort went toward one goal: that the student might know and interpret the Scripture correctly. Though very few actually became teachers, Scripture was absolutely central to education. It would be unthinkable for any teacher to attempt to undermine the very foundation that Jewish culture was built on.[8]

How does our church's approach to biblical education compare to this ancient Jewish system?

How would you rank the importance of studying Scripture in your own life?

Does seeing Jesus as an academic change your perception of Him?

"No," Jesus said, "I am not here to undermine the law." Then He continued: "In fact, I am raising the standard that many of you already consider to be too high." And that is just what He did. Jesus spent the next 88 verses raising the already high standard of the law (Matthew 5:21-7:27).

Before this sermon, the people who gathered there were able to confine things like murder and adultery and divorce and revenge in neat, little categories. But Jesus wiped all of that system away, saying that it was not enough just to refrain from the act of murder. Nope, if you hold onto anger against someone, then that's the same as if you actually kill someone. Likewise, adultery was no longer about a sexual act; it was now about looking at someone with lust. In light of this, it's no wonder that Jesus said in verse 20, "Unless your righteousness surpasses that of the scribes and Pharisees, you will never enter the kingdom of heaven."

Really comforting, Jesus. It's statements like that which bring all kinds of questions to mind: *I thought this whole thing was about grace and not works? Since when is entering the kingdom of heaven about obtaining a level of righteousness anyway? And while we're at it, just who are these guys who we're supposed to exceed in our level of righteousness?*

GETTING TO KNOW THE PHARISEES

The Pharisees get a bad name, and much of it is deserved. They did, after all, conspire and help to instigate the crucifixion. That's got to warrant some bad press. Their bad reputation is compounded because of their long-standing persona in religious history of being notoriously legalistic, so much so that they could not stomach the kind of freedom and newness that Jesus promised He was inaugurating. But let's not stop there. As is the case with most people, there is another side to the story of the Pharisees, and we need to look at that if we're really going to understand the comparison that Jesus made in these verses in Matthew.

The Pharisees were not a group who just happened to be roaming the streets of Israel during that time. Their sect was formed centuries earlier for a very specific purpose. The nation of Israel had been founded as a people who would have a unique relationship with Yahweh. He promised to pour out blessings on them as a people, reveal Himself in special ways to them, and treasure them as His own. In return they were to spread their blessings around the ancient world and be solely devoted to Yahweh as their God (Genesis 12:1-3). The laws were given as an extension of this covenant, or agreement.

While God unquestionably lived up to His end, the people did not. Time and time again, God's people chose to disobey direct commands that He had given them, most grievously in the form of worshiping idols. Such was the case for literally hundreds of years until finally—after many warnings from prophets—the punishments that were also outlined in the terms of the covenant (most notably in Deuteronomy 28) came to pass.

In what the Israelites would have considered an absolutely unthinkable act, God used a pagan army to judge His own people. In 586 B.C., the Babylonians ransacked Jerusalem, conquering the Jews and taking many of them away from their homeland as prisoners. The land God had promised them was gone. The temple and priestly system were eliminated. The temple itself was sacked. The centerpieces of religious and cultural life were decimated, and the result was catastrophic for the Israelites. Their foundations had been destroyed, and nothing was certain anymore.

When the Jewish people eventually were able to come back to their homeland, they had to face up to the hard fact that they had been exiled because they were not obedient to God's law. So a group formed and committed themselves thoroughly to studying, teaching, and observing the law so that they would never incur God's anger to that extent again.

These were not super-religious people. They were real-life, working-class, ordinary folks with no extraordinary religious education. They were, however, single-mindedly committed to one thing: keeping the law. These were the Pharisees. Not necessarily the evil, legalistic, conspirators we think of—just a group of people who didn't want to lose their homeland again.

What is your image of the Pharisees? Where does that picture come from?

Is it easier for you to judge the Pharisees or relate to them? Why?

Who would you say are the Pharisees in our churches today?

In what ways are you like a Pharisee? How are you unlike
a Pharisee?

DEFINING THE LAW

In order to keep the law, the Pharisees knew that the law had to be clearly
defined. So in addition to the written law of Moses, they built a kind of
hedge with their own verbal laws. The purpose was to ensure that the
written law was implemented in the right ways at the right times. By the
time of Jesus, the Jews had codified all of the Old Testament Scriptures so
that there were 613 laws. To those laws they also added hundreds of oral
rules, regulations, and traditions—so that even in the most specific area of
life, the rightness or wrongness of an action could be determined by a rule.
Exodus 31:15, for example, lays down a rule about the seventh day of the
week, declaring it a day dedicated to the Lord.

Therefore, everyone must refrain from work on the Sabbath. But what does
it really mean to work? The Pharisees wanted to figure that out, so they
divided work into 39 categories. One forbidden labor was plowing on the
Sabbath. To get even more specific, though, a person did not have to use
an actual plow to break this rule: If someone stood up from a chair and the
legs made a furrow in the ground, he could be accused of plowing on
the Sabbath.

The Mishnah (literally,
"repetition") is the
collection of Oral Torah
compiled and passed
down verbally through the
centuries. The Mishnah
records the sayings of
teachers who lived and
taught throughout the
centuries, both before and
after the time of Jesus.
It was not compiled and
committed to writing
until about 200 A.D., but is
nevertheless considered
to be just as inspired
as the written Torah in
Judaism.[9]

Perhaps now we can grasp the difficulty of what Jesus was asking when He said to the crowd of Matthew 5 that their righteousness must surpass the righteousness that comes from obeying even the most specific laws. I bet that stopped the whispers. I bet those people who were so excited about this new teacher were not so fired up anymore. If we're honest, we're not exactly fired up either. After all, isn't Christianity supposed to be about grace instead of works? Isn't it supposed to be about relationship instead of rules? Yet if we are reading this right, then Jesus has just said that those 613 laws of the Pharisees are not enough. In short, what He pretty much said was everyone must be perfect.

And it is in that moment we experience the discouraging feeling in our stomachs, probably much like His original audience did. And if we are suddenly panicked because the awful truth has hit us that we can never do all those things—that we can never do enough—then we are ready to hear the voice of the Lord say, "Do not be discouraged. Yes, it is true, I am the new lawgiver—the new Moses—but all I am doing right now is giving you the true meaning of the law. I am fulfilling the law by teaching it to you rightly."

If you were to measure your righteousness by obeying even the smallest of rules, how would you measure up?

What do you think Jesus meant by His statements about "greater righteousness"?

How do we tend to compare our righteousness to others?

The scribes were not only the recorders of the text of Scripture; they were also acknowledged to be the teachers, interpreters, and preservers of the law. The Pharisees were members of a sect committed to fulfilling the demands of Scripture through their elaborate oral tradition. Their strict obedience had become legendary by the time of Jesus.

Do you think God really wants us to compare our righteousness to others? If not, then what do you think Jesus means in this passage?

TO FULFILL

"To abolish" means to loose what had been bound or fastened; to dissolve, demolish, destroy, or throw down. Jesus did not come to abolish the law. Instead, He came to fulfill it. Now there's an interesting word. It's a word that is used in other places in the New Testament in very different situations. In Matthew 13:48, it describes a net being filled with fish. In John 12:3, it's associated with a perfumed smell filling a house. The word is used to describe a valley that's being filled in Luke 3:5. These examples illustrate an interesting point.

A net, a house, and a valley are all sorts of containers; there is nothing deficient in and of themselves because being empty is not a deficiency; it is their purpose to be empty so that they can be filled.

Enter Jesus, who declares that the law is not deficient. It is not lacking. It does exactly what it has always been meant to do—to serve as a container for the filling that God would provide in the form of Christ. The law was never intended to be the means by which people make themselves acceptable to God; it was always meant to point people to Jesus. For through Him comes the filling.

Jesus "filled" the law in the sense that He not only adhered to its external demands, but He also did so for right reasons with a right heart—making Him unique in universal history. The great fallacy of the Pharisees was not their commitment or their zeal; it was that in the midst of their zeal, they became so focused on outward actions that they neglected the inner righteousness that the law actually called for.

At its core, "righteousness" does not mean conformity to an enormous list of moral requirements; it's the inner quality that makes a person truly right and good. What Jesus called for is not list keeping but a heart that, at its core, is so good that it inevitably reflects righteousness in daily living. That's why Jesus expanded the law: He was reminding people that righteousness

"The law, then, was our guardian until Christ, so that we could be justified by faith. But since that faith has come, we are no longer under a guardian, for you are all sons of God through faith in Christ Jesus" (Galatians 3:24-26).

is a state that permeates one's whole being. He wanted to point out a distinction: It is people who are righteous, not people who do righteous things who God finds acceptable.

> **What is the difference between people who *are* and people who *do*?**

> **Why would God value one over the other?**

> **Which do you think you are? Why do you say that?**

> **How can we become "people who are"?**

SOME CHILDREN'S STORIES

Am I just splitting hairs here? What does it mean that God is after righteous people and not just people who do righteous things? For starters, it means that Jesus' approach to righteousness is radically different from that of the Pharisees. It is the difference between an outside/in mentality and an inside/out mentality. It is the difference between Pinocchio righteousness and Ugly Duckling righteousness.

Just to refresh your memory, the story of Pinocchio began with a carpenter named Gepetto. Out of his great sadness and loneliness, he constructed a puppet from wood and named it Pinocchio. While having a puppet was nice, it still served as a sore reminder of the old man's solitude. So Gepetto wished one night that Pinocchio would come to life, and the Blue Fairy came down and granted his wish. Pinocchio was a walking, talking, singing, dancing boy.

The only problem was that he was not a real boy—he was just a wooden boy acting like a real boy. Pinocchio himself wanted to be a real boy so badly that one night he wished upon a star that he would become real. The Blue Fairy visited him, and though Pinocchio did a fair job of messing up the Fairy's advice to "be a good puppet," he eventually ended up giving his own life to save his father's. For that act of heroism, the Blue Fairy decided that Pinocchio had at last proven himself worthy of growing his own skin and bones. So at last, through great effort and sacrifice, Pinocchio became what he was so desperately trying to be.

But the Ugly Duckling did not have that kind of experience. Born into a family of ducks, the Ugly Duckling wanted nothing more than to be a regular duck. But no matter how hard he tried, his feathers wouldn't become soft, his quack wouldn't sound right, and his neck wouldn't shrink. He was ridiculed in his duckling-hood because he looked different than the other ducks did, and he was left alone to fend for himself.

The real change came when the Ugly Duckling was just about ready to throw in the towel. He gazed morosely into the water one day and caught a glimpse of his own reflection. What he saw surprised him. His neck wasn't long; it was graceful. His feathers were spread down evenly across his back. He looked almost regal. He realized that he wasn't a duck, but a swan. Then his actions changed.

He flew gracefully. He glided majestically across the water. He was no longer trying to be something he was not; instead, he had realized his identity and was then very naturally living it out.

> **What differences do you see between the Ugly Duckling and Pinocchio?**

Kyle Strobel writes about the nature of real life change in Christ. His book, *Metamorpha*, challenges some previously held ideas about the nature of life with Jesus.

How do these stories relate to the kind of righteousness that Jesus wants in us?

RIGHTEOUS PEOPLE (AND TREES)

Much in the same way, Jesus doesn't hand us a list of rules and tell us that if we are able to keep all of them, then we'll be righteous and suitable for life in the kingdom. Instead, Jesus makes a tremendous offer: an exchange. He will take our sin and give us His own righteousness. And when we choose to accept His offer, then the Holy Spirit uproots the person we currently are. "Uprooted" maybe the best word for what happens in that exchange, especially when you consider what Jesus said about trees in Matthew 12:33-37.

Take a look at Matthew 12:33-37.
What principle do you think Jesus is getting at in this passage?

It's a simple observation with profound implications. The agricultural point Jesus made was nothing more complex than this—an apple tree produces apples. That's it. But let's just say that you don't like apples; you like oranges. The solution for your problem is not to go find an orange tree, pull the oranges off, and then duct tape them to the apple tree in your yard. The solution is to uproot the apple tree, throw it away, and plant a new kind of tree in its place.

In this passage, Jesus reminded the Pharisees that their problem was not necessarily that they were speaking evil things; it ran much deeper than that. Just like an apple tree producing apples, the Pharisees were only acting in accordance with their nature. Their nature was the problem; it's the root that's the issue. And that's what Jesus' sacrifice on the cross takes care of. In our current religious culture, we have relegated salvation to being about heaven and hell; it's something that really takes effect when you die. Not so, according to Jesus. It's about way more than that. It's about your core identity—the kind of tree you are on the inside. It's about the Holy Spirit using His cosmic backhoe to dig up the tree of your life and replace it with something new. That part is key for us.

Because of Christ, all our sin is taken away, but we are not left with some gaping hole. No, Jesus gives us His righteousness. Suddenly we are not God's enemy but His child. We are not criminals but ambassadors. And He is not our opponent but our Father. Everything has changed, and it's because Jesus has given us His righteousness. Then we realize the truth that Paul wrote about in 2 Corinthians 5:21—that God "made the One who did not know sin to be sin for us, so that we might become the righteousness of God in Him." He wrote about it again in Romans 8:4, saying that the law's requirements are "accomplished in us."

The implications are amazing. Suddenly we are not trying to be acceptable to God, but we are resting in the fact that we are already accepted. Even further, every time we choose to do the right thing, we are living as the people we truly are. That means that when we sin we are acting like someone we used to be. To put it in theological terms, we are no longer sinners but saints who happen to occasionally sin.

Perhaps it sounds too simple, but I believe that most of us have not yet accepted our own acceptance. That is to say, we spend the bulk of our life with Jesus feeling like we are a disappointment to God because of our actions. We live in a constant state of guilt, somehow believing that the worse we feel about ourselves, the more spiritual—or at the least, humble—we are. But where is the freedom in that? The peace? The joy? It's nowhere to be found.

Life with Christ is not about proving something; it's about accepting that something has already been proven by Him. We are not trying to be more righteous than the Pharisees. We already are. Maybe we should stop trying our best to produce oranges and realize that we have already been made into an orange tree.

What leads us to think that God is disappointed in us?

> "Faith is the courage to accept your own acceptance."
> —Paul Tillich

What are some ways we can base our relationship with Christ more on who we are than what we do?

Does focusing on who we are release us from obligations of moral conduct? Why do you say that?

"I press on to take hold of that for which Christ Jesus took hold of me. Brothers, I do not consider myself yet to have taken hold of it. But one thing I do: Forgetting what is behind and straining toward what is ahead, I press on toward the goal to win the prize for which God has called me heavenward in Christ Jesus. All of us who are mature should take such a view of things. And if on some point you think differently, that too God will make clear to you. Only let us live up to what we have already attained" (Philippians 3:12-16, NIV).

OK, so if we're already righteous, then why do so many churches, pastors, and books teach a spirituality that is little more than behaviorism? Though the answers are many, I think it might be because conduct is so much easier to quantify. We don't know what to do with a gospel that puts everyone on even footing, first as sinners and then as saints. With God, it's not a ladder but a plane; but it's frankly much easier to use a gauge to measure our life with Christ. And while we have that in the form of the Holy Spirit, we do not have a checklist by which we can hold up our spiritual accomplishments to God and everyone else.

Maybe we need to accept the completeness of what Christ did instead of living as if we are trying to gain what has already been given to us. Maybe we need to embrace that we are embraced. Maybe we need to behold that we are beholden. Maybe we need to accept that we are accepted. And in so doing, maybe we need to live in absolute freedom, knowing that all has been finished in Christ. Consider the magnitude of what was accomplished on the cross. Are you living like "it is finished," or are you living like you still have something to prove? If the answer is the latter, then do you really think Jesus needs your help to accomplish the complete saving and redemption of His people?

Rest. Rest in His work, not your own. Rest in His righteousness that has been given to you; the kind of righteousness that surpasses that of even the Pharisees; the kind of righteousness that works from the inside out.

- You can learn a lot from children's stories. How about taking a break from life this week and just watching a Disney movie?

- Sit alone with your journal this week. As you think over your experience with *Tough Sayings*, are there particular things you want to remember? Write about them. You might even want to share them with your small group.

- Send some e-mails to your group members telling them specific things they have said or done during your study together that have been meaningful to you.

NOTES

NOTES

ENDNOTES

SESSION 1

1. Spiros Zodhiates, *The Complete Word Study New Testament* (Chattanooga: AMG Publishers, 1992), 925.

2. *The Zondervan Pictorial Encyclopedia of the Bible,* Merrill Tenney, ed. (Grand Rapids: Zondervan, 1976), s. vv. "oil."

SESSION 2

3. *The Zondervan Pictorial Encyclopedia of the Bible,* Merrill Tenney, ed. (Grand Rapids: Zondervan, 1976), s. vv. "fig."

4. *http://rationalchristianity.net/fig_tree.html*

5. William Barclay, *The Gospel of Mark* (Philadelphia: The Westminster Press, 1975), 273.

SESSION 3

6. George R. Beasley-Murray, *Word Biblical Commentary: John* (Nashville: Thomas Nelson, 1999), 189.

7. David Stern, *Jewish New Testament Commentary* (Clarksville: Jewish New Testament Publications, 1992), 190.

SESSION 4

8. David Bivin, *New Light on the Difficult Words of Jesus* (Holland: En-Gedi Resource Center, 2005), 3.

9. Bivin, 158.

THE TOUGH SAYINGS OF JESUS

Michael Kelley

Table of Contents

Redefining Jesus?

What images come to your mind when you hear or see the name Jesus?

We come from different backgrounds, knowledge bases, and experiences. All those things influence our perceptions, even our perceptions of the same Scriptures we've read about who Jesus is.

The Bible refers to Jesus as the Alpha and Omega, the Lamb slain before the foundation of the world, and the Savior of the world. In the first chapter of John, He is the Word that was with God, and yet was God, from the beginning. The Gospels (Matthew, Mark, Luke, and John) say He is the Son, the Shepherd, and Seeker of the lost. But how do those descriptions play out in our understanding? We may use the same terms, but until we talk it through, we can't be sure if our understanding of those words really mesh.

That's why it's good for us to look at Scripture together. According to the Bible, Jesus has existed throughout history, whether as the mysterious fourth figure in the fiery furnace story of the Old Testament book of Daniel, or as the seemingly blasphemous miracle worker of the New Testament gospels. The image of the person may change, but the essence of who He is remains the same. It is that essence that we will dive into during this study.

THROUGH A NEW LENS

We also see Jesus through different lenses in different seasons of our lives. C.S. Lewis puts great words to this in his Chronicles of Narnia series. The novels present a Christ-figure in the form of a lion named Aslan in a country called Narnia. At one point in the stories, the youngest character, Lucy, returns to Narnia after some time away. She tells Aslan that he is bigger than when she left. Aslan wisely explains that he seems bigger to her, not because he has grown, but because *she* has: "Every year you grow, you will find me bigger." And so it is with our view of Jesus. Our experiences don't change who He is, but they do give us a different vantage point as we, with the guidance of the Holy Spirit, revisit what we understand about Him.

If you grew up going to church, your understanding of Jesus may have been built with macaroni art and felt-board stories. The pictures you saw might have portrayed a generous man with a welcoming smile full of love and compassion. You were probably taught that Jesus loved us and wanted to live inside of us. In this way, many of us began our relationship with Him.

For some, though, the relationship stayed within the confines of that scenario. The relationship did not grow as we grew. Our knowledge of Him remained very simple while our lives became increasingly complex. For those of us, it's very possible that this trimmed-down version of the Son of God has been bursting at the seams to escape the small understanding our minds and hearts have created for Him.

It's very possible that this trimmed-down version of the Son of God has been bursting at the seams to escape the small understanding our minds and hearts have created for Him.

THE RULE OF EXPANSION

Relationships are dynamic. They are a give-and-take process as time goes on; years after beginning a relationship with someone, we look back at the early days and wonder if we really knew the person at all back then. Why should our relationship with Christ be any different?

As wonderful as a growing relationship with a living God may sound and seem, there is an uncomfortable element to the continual reformation it requires. As we allow Jesus to burst through the macaroni frame and leap off the felt board, we may not always be comfortable. We may not be so sure we knew Jesus at all back then. Some parts of His ministry may not only be difficult to understand, but downright troubling.

Let's navigate these waters, even if they test our comfort zones. We cannot escape the fact that we don't completely understand everything Jesus said. But if we are to be in an authentic, growing relationship with Him, we need to explore what we don't understand. Have you avoided certain passages of the Bible because you didn't understand them or they didn't jive with the Jesus you've come to accept? Consider the following: Did Jesus look down on non-Jews? Was He a racist? Did He dishonor His family and ask His followers to do the same? Did Jesus teach about grace through faith, like the rest of the New Testament, or was He more about us proving our love for Him through our actions? These are some of the questions we'll explore in this study.

Hopefully, this experience will help us to face head-on what Scripture teaches—and doesn't teach—about Jesus' life and ministry. If we can revisit what the Bible says, then we can compare what we understand (or misunderstand) the facts to mean. Many of us have staked our faith on Christ. It is up to us, then, to revisit from time to time what we have put our faith in and whether what we've experienced in life has given us a greater ability to understand the truth about Jesus.

THE BEAUTY IN DOUBT
Sometimes an over-simplified view of faith can leave us with the idea that we should shy away from the tough questions out of fear that our faith could be injured. Before we proceed with the study, let's define faith.

In some theological vocabularies, *faith* is represented as "the absence of doubt." With that definition, the measure of how much faith we have is determined by how little doubt accompanies it.

But is there really anything in our lives that doesn't contain a certain measure of doubt or at least questioning? Unfortunately, an over-simplified definition of faith doesn't leave room for questions, so we end up living with closeted doubt that only shows its face during the most grim and troubling times in our lives.

There is a more realistic—and more authentic—way to approach faith and doubt. Our definition of faith should be more than the absence of doubt; instead, doubt can be an essential element to the process of faith. We have faith in something bigger than our doubts and questions. We don't have to fear them. If we can push hard into our questions instead of hiding them, we trust God to be bigger. And He is. God is big enough to receive us, doubt and all. Doubts and questions do not counter faith; instead, they should push us deeper.

Let's embrace authentic faith. Let's look at all that we know about Christ, even the parts we can't completely figure out. Let's let Him speak to us through what the Bible teaches, even if we don't completely understand. Even when, as in the Scripture for Session 1, it seems He tells a self-righteous young man that the key to salvation is not faith at all—but works . . .

Listen to the audio file "Conflict Insulation." It will come via e-mail from your group leader. Think about the following questions as you listen and come to your group's first study lesson ready to discuss your thoughts.

- How does our avoidance of conflict relate to our faith?
- How do we try to insulate our faith in a "comfortable fortress of security"?
- How does navigating through doubt actually strengthen our faith?

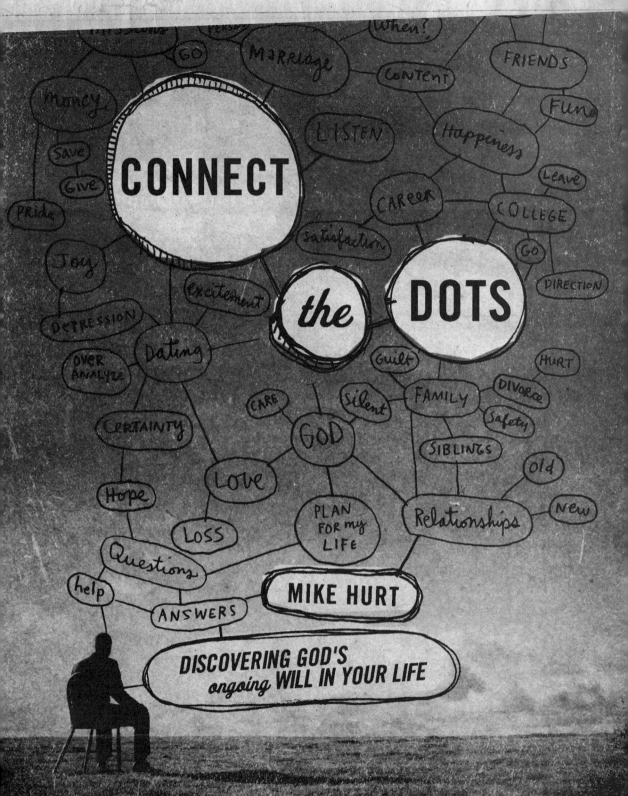

CONNECT the DOTS

MIKE HURT

DISCOVERING GOD'S ongoing WILL IN YOUR LIFE

TABLE of CONTENTS

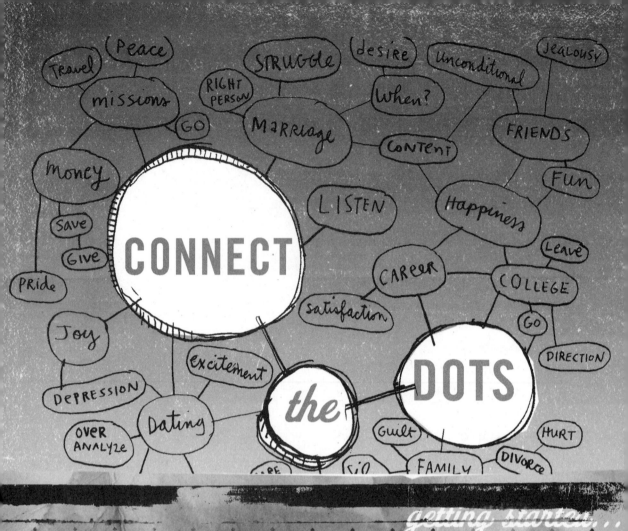

BEYOND THE BIG THREE

NOTHING SEEMS TO MOTIVATE A SEARCH FOR HIGHER PURPOSE THAN THE "BIG THREE." AS A PASTOR, I HAVE BEEN MEETING WITH YOUNG ADULTS FOR 15 YEARS. DURING THAT TIME, I HAVE LEARNED THAT THE BIG THREE . . .

WHO SHOULD I MARRY? WHERE SHOULD I WORK? AND WHERE SHOULD I LIVE?—CONSISTENTLY MOVE PEOPLE TO START ASKING THE SEEMINGLY SIMPLE QUESTION: "WHAT IS GOD'S WILL FOR MY LIFE?"

If you are asking these questions, you are certainly not alone—especially if you have spent a couple of years in the workplace and are wondering where you go from here. These are natural questions to ask; it's a part of growing in wisdom. It's a part of defining how you are going to live your life. It's a part of learning what it means to be you on your terms.

But perhaps that is also the flaw in the big three questions. It seems to me that we want to know God's will as long as His will lines up nicely with our idea of what our life should generally be like. That's usually why the big three prompt us to ask the question of God's will—we have in our minds and hearts what we want the answer to be. If that is true, then our question is not really, "What is God's will for my life?" Instead, it's "Does God's will for my life line up with my vision for my life?"

The result is a jumbled blend of our ideas and God's ideas, our desires and His desires, our will and His will. Further complicating the situation is the reality that very few of us have ever seen the proverbial skywriting telling us exactly where to work or who to marry. Many more of us have asked for God to answer our big life questions, but at the end of the day, we have simply had to make a decision with little more than a sense of which direction God wants us to go. The search for any amount of certainty or confidence in God's will has become little more than a pipe dream for most of us. Like a carrot just out of reach of the horse's nose, we ask these big questions hoping to hear a cosmic voice affirm some direction, and yet that voice always seems to be just out of earshot.

Despite this, I firmly believe that God cares deeply about the big decisions of your life. Furthermore, I believe He is incredibly concerned about the mundane, ordinary moments of your life—so much so that perhaps the question God wants us to ask is slightly different than the one we are asking right now.

MAYBE, BECAUSE GOD WANTS TO BE INTIMATELY INVOLVED IN EVERY DETAIL OF YOUR LIFE, THE QUESTION WE SHOULD BE ASKING IS NOT, "WHAT IS GOD'S WILL *FOR* MY LIFE?" BUT "WHAT IS GOD'S WILL *IN* MY LIFE?"

The difference is huge. If you are asking for God's will for your life, then you are looking for a crystal ball. You want to see into the future to try and find the most prosperous way to go. But if you recognize that God's will is not only *for* your life but *in* your life, then you are choosing to believe in a God who is more than just a fortune-teller. You are choosing to believe that God's greatest call is not for you to be married or single, a preacher or a doctor, to live in Miami or Beijing. His greatest call is for you to follow Jesus—every moment.

Maybe the next several weeks can be a time for you to rediscover that God doesn't just have a plan for you but that God cares deeply about you. Sometimes in the discussion of God's will, we can lose sight of God's love and kindness. If all we are looking for is God's will for our lives, then we betray our perception of God. Our questions reveal that we believe that God is very interested in what we do, where we go, and what we can accomplish on His behalf in the world. But is He only interested in us to the extent that we can be useful to Him?

But I believe God is much more interested in who we are than what we do. For this reason, we do not seek to find answers as much as we seek to find God Himself. It is only through our journey together with Him that we find answers, but amazingly, those answers will become of secondary importance to the great joy and satisfaction of just walking in relationship with God.

That's why it's so vital that we are convinced of God's love for us. Much in the same way that we do not just want answers from Him, He does not just want performance from us. We are meant for each other—us and God—and not just so that we can accomplish each other's desires. We are meant to walk with each other. We are meant to be in each other's lives. We are meant to live deeply together.

I hope that, for you, the end result of *Connect the Dots* is a greater love for, hope in, and commitment to the will of God in your life.

WHAT IS THREADS?

WE ARE A COMMUNITY OF YOUNG ADULTS—
people who are piecing the Christian life together, one
experience at a time. Threads is driven by four key markers
that are essential to young adults everywhere, and though
it's always dangerous to categorize people, we think these
are helpful in reminding us why we do what we do.

First of all, we are committed to being *responsible*. That is,
doing the right thing. Though we're trying to grow in our
understanding of what that is, we're glad we already know
what to do when it comes to recycling, loving our neighbor,
tithing, or giving of our time.

Community is also important to us. We believe we all need
people. People we call when the tire's flat and people we call
when we get the promotion. And it's those people—the day-
in-day-out people—that we want to walk through life with.

Then there's *connection*. A connection with our church, a connection with somebody
who's willing to walk along side us and give us a little advice here and there. We'd like a
connection that gives us the opportunity to pour our lives out for somebody else—and
that whole walk along side us thing, we're willing to do that for someone else, too.

And finally there's *depth*. Kiddie pools are for kids. We're looking to dive in, head first,
to all the hard-to-talk-about topics, the tough questions, and heavy Scriptures. We're
thinking this is a good thing, because we're in process. We're becoming. And who
we're becoming isn't shallow.

We're glad you're here. Be sure and check us out online at:

THREADSMEDIA.COM

**STOP BY TO JOIN OUR ONLINE COMMUNITY —
AND COME BY TO VISIT OFTEN!**

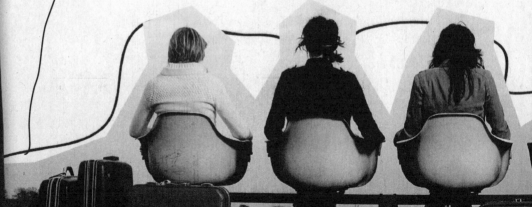

GET UNCOMFORTABLE:
SERVE THE POOR. STOP INJUSTICE.
CHANGE THE WORLD … IN JESUS' NAME.
BY TODD PHILLIPS

Phillips guides you to understand how your faith in Christ and concern for the poor go hand-in-hand. As he examines God's character and perspective regarding poverty and injustice, he offers an understanding of what God calls you to do, along with practical ways to impact culture by caring for "the least of these."

TODD PHILLIPS *is the teaching pastor of Frontline, the young adult ministry of McLean Bible Church near Washington D.C. His passions are teaching the people of God and sharing the Gospel with those who aren't yet Christians. He is the author of* Spiritual CPR: Reviving a Flat-lined Generation.

JADED:
REDISCOVERING HOPE IN REALITY
BY MIKE HARDER

Harder's second study with Threads walks people through the difference between our expectations of life and reality. *Jaded* offers hope to those who have been wounded by their experiences and provides concret ways to choose hope in Christ rather than cynicism.

MIKE HARDER *is the co-pastor of Green Hills Church in Nashville, Tennessee, as well as a speaker guy and ministry consultant. through his speaking, writing, and teaching, Mike is motivated by the opportunity to impact the spiritual condition of the people in his generation.*

THE EXCHANGE:
TIRED OF LIVING THE CHRISTIAN LIFE ON YOUR OWN?
BY JOEL ENGLE

An exploration of Romans 6, 7, and 8, this study will help you understand that the power of the Christian life is not found in yourself or religious activity, but in "exchanging" your life for the life of Jesus Christ. You'll learn how to overcome sin and personal hang-ups through a life of dependency on Christ.

JOEL ENGLE *is a worship communicator who uses his gifts to impact lives and glorify God. In* The Exchange, *Joel shares his own story of finally understanding what the Christian life is all about and learning to depend solely on Christ.*

GROUP CONTACT INFORMATION

Name _____ Number _____
Email _____

Name _____ Number _____
Email _____

Name _____ Number _____
Email _____

Name _____ Number _____
Email _____

Name _____ Number _____
Email _____

Name _____ Number _____
Email _____

Name _____ Number _____
Email _____

Name _____ Number _____
Email _____

Name _____ Number _____
Email _____

Name _____ Number _____
Email _____